1 Year of Sunday School Lessons for 3-5 Year Olds

Angela E. Powell

Copyright © 2015 Angela E. Powell

Verses quoted in this text have been taken from the HOLY BIBLE: EASY-TO-READ VERSION © 2001 by World Bible Translation Center, Inc. and used by permission.

Other verses quoted in this text have been taken from The Living Bible copyright © 1971 by Tyndale House Foundation. Used by permission of Tyndale House Publishers Inc., Carol Stream, Illinois 60188. All rights reserved. The Living Bible, TLB, and the The Living Bible logo are registered trademarks of Tyndale House Publishers.

Scriptures taken from the Holy Bible, New International Version®, NIV®. Copyright © 1973, 1978, 1984, 2011 by Biblica, Inc.™ Used by permission of Zondervan. All rights reserved worldwide. www.zondervan.com The "NIV" and "New International Version" are trademarks registered in the United States Patent and Trademark Office by Biblica, Inc.™

All images contained in this text, with the exception of the cover photo are © Angela E. Powell

All rights reserved. The purchase of this material entitles the buyer to reproduce lessons and activities for classroom use only – not for commercial resale. Reproduction of these materials for an entire school or district is prohibited. No part of this book may be reproduced (except as noted above), stored in a retrieval system, or transmitted in any form or by any means (mechanically, electronically, recording, etc.) without the prior written consent of Angela E. Powell.   Printed in the USA

ISBN-10: 0-9991594-0-2
ISBN-13: 978-0-9991594-0-8

DEDICATION

To all the precious preschoolers God has brought into my life over the years. Without you, this book never would have been possible.

TABLE OF CONTENTS

HOW TO USE THIS BOOK 1
J A N U A R Y 3
   LESSON 1: CREATION OF THE WORLD 4
   LESSON 2: CREATION OF MAN 10
   LESSON 3: THE 23RD PSALM 14
   LESSON 4: THE 10 PLAGUES 18
   LESSON 5: JOSEPH BECOMES A MIGHTY RULER 22
      JANUARY MEMORY VERSE CARDS 28
F E B R U A R Y 29
   LESSON 1: WHAT IS LOVE? 1 CORINTHIANS 13 30
   LESSON 2: THE 10 COMMANDMENTS 35
   LESSON 3: JESUS CALLS THE CHILDREN 40
   LESSON 4: LOVING OTHERS 44
   LESSON 5: THE GOOD SAMARITAN 47
      FEBRUARY MEMORY VERSE CARDS 50
M A R C H 51
   LESSON 1: ADAM & EVE: THE FIRST SIN 52
   LESSON 2: PALM SUNDAY 55
   LESSON 3: THE LAST SUPPER 58
   LESSON 4: JESUS' DEATH & RESURRECTION 63
   LESSON 5: WHAT JESUS DID WHILE IN THE GRAVE 66
      MARCH MEMORY VERSE CARDS 69
A P R I L 70
   LESSON 1: DAVID & GOLIATH 71
   LESSON 2: SAMSON 74
   LESSON 3: GOD'S ARMOR FOR US 77
   LESSON 4: GIDEON THE SCARED SOLDIER 81
   LESSON 5: JOSHUA AND THE BIG WALL 84
      APRIL MEMORY VERSE CARDS 87
M A Y 88
   LESSON 1: THE LORD'S PRAYER 89
   LESSON 2: DANIEL & THE LIONS 95
   LESSON 3: HANNAH'S PRAYER 98
   LESSON 4: PAUL IN PRISON 101
   LESSON 5: ELIJAH'S PRAYER & A CONTEST 104
      MAY MEMORY VERSE CARDS 107
J U N E 108
   LESSON 1: WHO IS THE HOLY SPIRIT? 109
   LESSON 2: THE DAY OF PENTECOST 112
   LESSON 3: HOW THE HOLY SPIRIT TALKS TO US 115
   LESSON 4: PRAYING IN THE SPIRIT 119
   LESSON 5: HOW THE HOLY SPIRIT HELPS US 123
      JUNE MEMORY VERSE CARDS 126

JULY 127
LESSON 1: WHAT IS FREEDOM? 128
LESSON 2: FREEDOM ISN'T FREE 132
LESSON 3: FREEDOM FROM SIN 136
LESSON 4: WHAT DOES FREEDOM IN CHRIST LOOK LIKE? 139
LESSON 5: HELPING OTHERS BE FREE 143
JULY MEMORY VERSE CARDS 146

AUGUST 147
LESSON 1: WHAT IS A FRIEND? 148
LESSON 2: JESUS IS OUR BFF 151
LESSON 3: ZACCHAEUS IN THE TREE 154
LESSON 4: JESUS HELPS HIS FRIENDS 157
LESSON 5: GOD'S FRIEND ABRAHAM 160
AUGUST MEMORY VERSE CARDS 163

SEPTEMBER 164
LESSON 1: JESUS HEALS A PARALYZED MAN 165
LESSON 2: JESUS GIVES HIS FRIENDS POWER TO HEAL 168
LESSON 3: JESUS HEALS A BLIND MAN 171
LESSON 4: JESUS HEALS A MAN'S DAUGHTER 174
LESSON 5: JESUS RAISES LAZARUS 177
SEPTEMBER MEMORY VERSE CARDS 180

OCTOBER 181
LESSON 1: JESUS' 12 HELPERS 182
LESSON 2: NOAH HELPS GOD SAVE THE WORLD 185
LESSON 3: ESTHER HELPS GOD SAVE THE JEWS 190
LESSON 4: HOW WE CAN BE GOD'S HELPERS 193
LESSON 5: PAUL HELPED JESUS SPREAD THE GOOD NEWS 196
OCTOBER MEMORY VERSE CARDS 199

NOVEMBER 200
LESSON 1: THE 10 LEPERS 201
LESSON 2: A THANKFUL HEART IS WILLING TO GIVE 204
LESSON 3: JEHOSHAPHAT DEFEATS AN ARMY 208
LESSON 4: BEING THANKFUL NO MATTER WHAT 211
LESSON 5: LET EVERYTHING THAT HAS BREATH PRAISE THE LORD ... 215
NOVEMBER MEMORY VERSE CARDS 217

DECEMBER 218
LESSON 1: GOD TALKS TO MARY & JOSEPH 219
LESSON 2: MARY & JOSEPH MAKE A LONG JOURNEY 222
LESSON 3: JESUS IS BORN 225
LESSON 4: WISE MEN BRING GIFTS TO JESUS 228
LESSON 5: JESUS IS THE BEST PRESENT TO GIVE OTHERS 231
DECEMBER MEMORY VERSE CARDS 233

REFERENCE GUIDE 234

HOW TO USE THIS BOOK

Thank you for purchasing this book! I know the preschoolers in your church will have loads of fun doing these lessons with you. The lessons have been taught and tweaked over the course of a year and a half with preschoolers ages 3 to 5. Below are some tips on using this curriculum.

TO BEGIN: This curriculum is flexible. You can skip sections, whole lessons, or do them out of order. Experiment with what works best in your classroom with your time restraints.

This book was designed for all churches and all budgets. Most, if not all of the items you will need can be bought at a dollar store or donated from families in your church. It doesn't matter if your class has 1 or 50 children, you can use this book. There are options for everyone.

THE OVERVIEW

Each month contains five lessons to choose from. The Overview Page shows the theme for the month, a description of each lesson, and the Memory Verse. You may find it helpful to copy the Overview Page and place it in your room so all your teachers can see it.

THE LESSONS

SUPPLIES NEEDED: Each lesson starts with a list of supplies. You may not need all of the items listed since you have several choices in how to teach each lesson.

LET'S PLAY A GAME: Each lesson offers games that tie into the scriptures being taught. As you play the games, use them to make a point about the lesson.

> **Individual Play** - Ideal for small groups of kids, but can be played with larger groups as well.

> **Multiple Play** - Ideal for large groups of kids or teams.

MEMORY VERSE: At the beginning of each month, have Memory Verse cards printed out for the children to take home and practice with their parents. Consider having a prize box as an incentive for kids to memorize scripture. One idea is to have the kids practice their verse all month and on the last Sunday, whoever can recite the verse, without help, can choose a prize.

LEARNING GOD'S WORD: Because children learn by doing, these hands-on lessons are meant to engage the kids. However, because teachers have preferences with regard to tidiness and activity level these lessons allow teachers to customize the lessons to fit their teaching styles. The important thing is to be excited about knowing God loves us and we can trust Him. When the teacher is enthusiastic about the lesson, the children will be drawn in.

HOW TO USE THIS BOOK

As part of the lesson, ask the kids some or all of the Discussion Questions to help them personalize God's truth. There are no answers to the questions in this book. This is because the questions are simply to get kids thinking about the story in ways they may not have before. This will also allow your teachers to get to know the kids better.

AN IMPORTANT NOTE: These lessons are meant to be used with a chapter and verse Bible, not a kid's story Bible. Choose one or two with simple language to keep in your classroom, and you won't have to struggle with different versions from different teachers.

DISCOVERING PRAYER: This section is a mini-lesson on prayer. Asking the questions will help the kids think about prayer in new ways and encourage them to pray for each other.

LET'S CREATE: Kids enjoy expressing their creativity. Most lessons have two or three options for crafts that can be made with basic, inexpensive supplies. **One thing to note:** There are no coloring pages. Even the crafts are designed to challenge little ones to think about God's word and serve to remind them about what they learned in class.

TO SUM UP

Have fun with this curriculum! Enjoy the energy children produce and learn from them as you watch them learn and grow in the things of God.

You may wonder why there isn't anything about praise and worship in this book. I would strongly suggest you include a short time of praise and worship in your class, but the songs and how you go about it are totally up to you.

The importance of effectively communicating God's Word to children cannot be minimized. This curriculum enables you to fulfill that assignment in creative ways that are fun for teachers and children alike.

If you have questions or comments about anything in this book, you can find my contact information in the back of this book on page 234.

Blessings,

Angela E. Powell

JANUARY
GOD HAS A PLAN FOR YOU

OVERVIEW

In these lessons, the children will learn through Bible stories that God created everyone for a purpose. Including them.

Memory Verse

Jeremiah 29:11

"I know the plans I have for you. Plans for good and not for evil."

Hand Motions

I know
Point to head.

The plans
Pretend to write on your hand like it's a piece of paper.

I have for you
Point to a friend.

Plans for good
Give a thumbs up.

And not for evil
Give a thumbs down.

LESSON 1: Creation of the World
God made the earth with us in mind. He created everything we would need. This lesson will explore what God created and the order God created them in. The children will see how God planned things for His people.

LESSON 2: Creation of Man
God created us to be unique. This lesson will explore how much planning God put into each of our bodies. The children will learn about fingerprints and why we have joints such as elbows and knees.

LESSON 3: The 23rd Psalm
The 23rd Psalm is one of the classics. This lesson will explore *when* God is with us. The children will discover that even in times when God doesn't feel near, He is always with them, no matter what.

LESSON 4: The 10 Plagues
God is a miracle worker! This lesson will explore the difference between God's will and our own. The children will learn that even though Pharaoh had a plan for the Hebrew people, God also had a plan for them and in the end, God won.

LESSON 5: Joseph Becomes a Mighty Ruler
Joseph's life seemed pretty rough, but he knew God had a plan for him. This lesson will explore how God can use bad things and turn them into good things. The children will learn that even if life doesn't seem fair, we can always trust God to help.

LESSON 1: CREATION OF THE WORLD

Supplies Needed for this Lesson:

Building Blocks	Play-Doh	Paint	Paper
Paint Brushes	Paint Smocks	Foam Board	Toy Plants
Cookie Cutters	Green Felt	Toy animals	Scissors
Blue Cellophane	Paper Plates	Colored Paper	Finger Paint
Popsicle Sticks	Crayons	Male and Female Figurines	Glue
Tape	Toy Trees	Pen	

Pictures of Sun, Moon, Clouds, Birds, Stars and Fish

LET'S PLAY A GAME!

Individual Play

Create an Animal with Blocks

Supplies Needed: Building blocks of various shapes and sizes or Play-Doh.

- Have the kids build their favorite animal or a wild animal. As they build ask them why they chose certain blocks, colors or shapes.
- Ask them if they made a plan about how they would build their animals or if they just made decisions as they went along.
- This exercise will get kids thinking about how they plan for things. This will let them relate their experiences with how God planned the earth for us.

Multiple Play

Memory Matching Game

Supplies Needed: Copies of the game pieces from pages 5 and 6. Cut out, mix up and place face down on a table or floor.

- Let each child take turns flipping over two cards. If they get a match, they can pick up their cards. If they don't, they have to flip the pieces back over again and wait until their next turn. Continue until all cards have been matched.
- Once the game is over ask the kids how they planned their next move.
- This exercise will allow the kids to relate their experiences with how God planned the earth for us.

1 Year of Sunday School Lessons for 3-5 year olds | Angela E. Powell

MEMORY GAME

For large groups of kids, make several copies and divide into teams. See which team can find all the matches first!

All Images © Angela E. Powell

5

MEMORY GAME

All Images © Angela E. Powell

MEMORY VERSE

Read the memory verse to the kids, showing them the hand motions to help them learn it. Have the kids repeat the verse with you a couple times while doing the hand motions.

I know - Point to your head.
The plans - Pretend to write on paper.
I have for you - Point to a friend.
Plans for good - Give a thumbs up.
And not for evil - Give a thumbs down.

> Copy and cut out the memory verse cards for this month so the kids can take them home to practice!

LET'S LEARN GOD'S WORD!

> **Teacher Preparation**
> Before class, choose one of the following Hands-On Activities for the kids to do while you read the story.

Paint a Mural
Supplies Needed: Paint, paper, paint smocks, water, brushes, and tape.
- Tape butcher paper to the wall, or give each child an individual piece of paper and tape them together later.
- Ask the kids to name some things God created.
- After the kids come up with a list, ask them to paint some of those things.
- Tell the kids to listen for other things God created as you read the story from a children's Bible and tell them they can paint those as well.

A Play-Doh World
Supplies Needed: Play-Doh, cookie cutters.
- Ask the kids to name some things God created.
- After the kids have come up with a list, ask them to begin creating some of those things out of Play-Doh.
- Tell the kids to listen for other things God created as you read them the story out of a children's Bible. Tell them they can build those things as well.

3-D Model of the World
Supplies Needed: Foam board, pictures of sun, moon, stars, birds and clouds glued to sticks, green felt, blue cellophane, toy trees, toy plants, cut-outs of fish, toy animals, one male and one female toy figurine.
- As you read each part of the story out of a children's Bible, let the kids make the world by sticking things on the foam board.

LET'S LEARN GOD'S WORD!

Read these verses out of a children's Bible while the kids do their hands-on activity. After reading the verses, engage the kids by asking questions about the text. Below are some questions to get you started.

Lesson Time Verses

Day 1: Genesis 1: 1-5
Day 2: Genesis 1: 6-8
Day 3: Genesis 1: 9-13
Day 4: Genesis 1: 14-19
Day 5: Genesis 1: 20-23
Day 6: Genesis 1: 24-31
Day 7: Genesis 2: 1-3

Discussion Questions

1. If you were going to make the sky what color would you make it?
2. How can you tell if it's night or day?
3. What do we call water from the sky?
4. What are your favorite fruits? What are your favorite veggies?
5. Did you know God made food because He knew we would enjoy it?
6. What do you think would have happened if God had created plants before he created water?
7. How many stars do you think God created?
8. Where does light come from?
9. Remember on the first day when God made light? This tells us God made the sun AFTER He made light. Why do you think that is?
10. What animals are your favorite? Did you know God made animals because He knew we would enjoy them?
11. God also provided us with food when he made animals. What kinds of food do we eat that comes from animals? Why do you think God made plants before he made animals?
12. God made humans last of all. Why do you think that is?
13. What would have happened if God had made humans before he made dry land?
14. What would have happened if God had made humans before he made food?
15. What did God do on the 7th day?
16. Why do you think God needed to rest?

DISCOVERING PRAYER!

Snack time can be a great time to teach preschoolers about prayer. You can also take prayer requests, review previous prayer requests, and receive praise reports.

1. What is another name for talking to God?
2. When can we pray?

LET'S CREATE!

Handprint Sun
Supplies Needed: Paper plates, yellow and orange paper, yellow and orange finger paint, and glue.
- Give each child a paper plate with their name written on the back.
- Help them trace their hand on the yellow and orange paper.
- Cut out several of their handprints.
- While you're cutting, let the kids use finger paint to paint the center of their plates.
- When the hands are all cut out, have the kids glue the handprints on the edge of the paper plate with the fingers facing out.
- Let the plates dry and hand to parents at the end of class.

Handprint Bird
Supplies Needed: Paper, pen, glue, crayons, and scissors.
- Trace both hands of each child, fingers spread out.
- Cut out the handprints.
- Have the kids glue the thumbs of each handprint together.
- Let the kids color their birds.

LESSON 2: CREATION OF MAN

Supplies Needed for this Lesson:

Small Box with Lid	Small Mirror	Paper	Crayons
Play-Doh	Paint	Paint Brushes	Paint Smocks
Cotton Balls	String	Stickers	Ink Pads
No-Bake Clay	Marker	Small Dowel Rod	

LET'S PLAY A GAME!

Individual Play

Who Made You Special?

Supplies Needed: Small box with lid, mirror.

- Before class, put a mirror in the bottom of the box.
- Have the children take turns guessing who is in the box.
- Tell the kids you will let them look in the box, but they can't say who is in the box.
- Allow the children to look in the box one at a time.
- After all the children have had a turn, ask them who was in the box.
- Explain that they are all important because God made them special.

Multiple Play

Different Faces

Supplies Needed: Paper and crayons.

- Give each child a piece of paper and have them draw one part of a face.
- Once they finish their part, have them pass their paper to the person next to them.
- Tell the kids to draw another face part on their friend's paper.
- Have them pass their papers again and repeat until every paper has a face.
- Point out how everyone decided to do their face parts in different ways. Even though the kids helped each other, all the faces look different.

MEMORY VERSE

Read the memory verse to the kids, showing them the hand motions to help them learn it. Have the kids repeat the verse with you a couple times while doing the hand motions.

I know - Point to your head.
The plans - Pretend to write on paper.
I have for you - Point to a friend.
Plans for good - Give a thumbs up.
And not for evil - Give a thumbs down.

> Copy and cut out the memory verse cards for this month so the kids can take them home to practice!

LET'S LEARN GOD'S WORD!

> **Teacher Preparation**
> Before class, choose one of the following Hands-On Activities for the kids to do while you read the story.

Play-Doh Person
Supplies Needed: Play-Doh.
- Let the kids choose a color of Play-Doh. As you read the story out of a children's Bible let them create a person.
- When the lesson is over, ask the kids why they chose that color and why they decided to put certain features on their people.
- Have the kids look at each other's projects and note the differences.
- Explain that God made us all unique, just like their projects are unique.

Create a Person
Supplies Needed: Paper, crayons, paint, water, brushes, string, cotton balls, and stickers.
- Decide if you want the kids to paint, color or create a person out of various objects that can be glued to the paper.
- Give each child a piece of paper.
- Tell them to create a person and use a lot of detail.
- When the lesson is over, ask the kids why they chose certain details.
- Have them look at each other's projects and note the differences.
- Explain that God made us all unique, just like all of their projects are unique.

Read these verses out of a children's Bible while the kids do their hands-on activity. After reading the verses, engage the kids by asking questions about the text. On the next page are some questions to get you started.

> **Lesson Time Verses**
> Genesis 1:26 – 2:3

LET'S LEARN GOD'S WORD!

Discussion Questions

1. Look at your hands. What do you see?
2. Why do you think we have lines on our hands?
3. Move and bend your fingers. Do you see how our fingers bend at those lines on our hands?
4. Look at your fingertips. Do you see all those really small lines?
5. Did you know all those small lines make-up our fingerprints? God gave each of us a different fingerprint. None of us here have the same one!
6. What else can we do with our hands? Why don't each of you go find one thing from the class and bring it back. How do each of your objects feel?
7. Now feel your elbows or knees. Do you think elbows and knees look kind of funny?
8. Do you know why God gave us elbows and knees?
9. If you didn't have any elbows do you think it would be easy or hard to get a drink of water?

DISCOVERING PRAYER!

Snack time can be a great time to teach preschoolers about prayer. You can also take prayer requests, review previous prayer requests, and receive praise reports.

1. Does God listen to us when we pray?
2. How do you know He listens?
3. What kind of future does God want us to have?

LET'S CREATE!

Fingerprint Flowers & Bugs
Supplies Needed: Paper, ink pads, crayons.
- Give each child a blank piece of paper.
- Set out ink pads on the table.
- Show the kids how to make a flower with your fingerprints.
- Explain that God created us so that no person has the exact same fingerprint.
- When the kids finish their pictures, have them look at all the fingerprints, and ask them if they can see the differences in each.

LET'S CREATE!

Fingerprint Necklace or Bracelet

Supplies Needed: No-bake clay, marker or crayon for each child, small dowel rod, ink pad, string, and a marker for the teacher.

- Give each child a small ball of no-bake clay.
- Let each child roll the clay into a small circle with a marker or crayon. Make sure it's not too thin.
- Once the clay is rolled out, have each child put a finger on an ink pad then press the finger into the clay.
- Make a hole in the top of the clay with a small dowel and set aside to dry.
- When the clay is dry, put a string through the hole and tie it.
- On the back of the fingerprint, you can write with a marker "God Made Me".

LESSON 3: THE 23RD PSALM

Supplies Needed for this Lesson:

Small Cups	Marshmallows	Paper Plates	Cotton Balls
Glue	Black Construction Paper	Scissors	Markers
Stapler	Crayons	Colored Construction Paper	

LET'S PLAY A GAME!

Individual Play

Follow the Leader through Psalm 23

Supplies Needed: None.

- Play follow the leader and have the kids follow you through Psalm 23.
- When you go by green pastures, roll on the floor like you're rolling down a hill.
- When you pass the calm waters, have them get a drink from the stream.
- When you walk through the dark valley, crawl on the floor.
- When the meal is prepared, pretend to eat.
- When welcomed as an honored guest, curtsey or take a bow.

Multiple Play

Overflowing Cup

Supplies Needed: Small cups, marshmallows or other soft items to fill the cups with.

- Divide the kids into groups of two.
- Have one person in each group lay on the floor.
- Give the person on the floor a cup to hold on their forehead.
- Have the other person stand at the head of the person on the floor.
- Give the person standing a small bowl of marshmallows.
- Have the kids drop marshmallows into the cup until it's full.
- The first group to fill their cup wins.
- Have the kids switch positions and play again.

MEMORY VERSE

Read the memory verse to the kids, showing them the hand motions to help them learn it. Have the kids repeat the verse with you a couple times while doing the hand motions.

I know - Point to your head.
The plans - Pretend to write on paper.
I have for you - Point to a friend.
Plans for good - Give a thumbs up.
And not for evil - Give a thumbs down.

> Copy and cut out the memory verse cards for this month so the kids can take them home to practice!

LET'S LEARN GOD'S WORD!

> **Teacher Preparation**
> Before class, choose one of the following Hands-On Activities for the kids to do while you read the story.

Imagination Station
Supplies Needed: None.
- As you read the 23rd Psalm to them out of a children's Bible, have the kids close their eyes and imagine themselves in the scenery.
- After each part, ask the kids to describe what they see and how they feel.
- After reading it through the first time, read it again. Only this time tell the kids to imagine Jesus is walking with them.
- After each part, ask the kids to describe how they feel and if Jesus made them feel any different from the last time.
- If some of the children are afraid of the dark valley, have them imagine that Jesus is holding their hand until they walk out of it.
- Ask them if they felt safer when Jesus was with them.

Sounds Around Us
Supplies Needed: None.
- Ask the kids to make different kinds of sounds, peaceful, scary, silly, calm, angry etc.
- Read each section of Psalm 23 to the kids out of a children's Bible.
- After each section ask the kids what kind of sounds would belong in that section.
- Ask the kids why they think those sounds would belong there.

LET'S LEARN GOD'S WORD!

Read these verses out of a children's Bible while the kids do their hands-on activity. After reading the verses, engage the kids by asking questions about the text. Below are some questions to get you started.

Lesson Time Verses
Psalm 23

Discussion Questions

1. When we imagine ourselves with Jesus, how does Jesus make us feel?
2. Do you think God wants us to be scared?
3. Did the dark valley seem scary?
4. Did the green pastures seem scary?
5. This week, if there is anything you're scared of, do you think you can try to remember God is always with us and wants good things for us?
6. Do you think if we remember God is with us it will help us to not be so scared?
7. Do you know what it means when it says "My cup overflows"?
8. God wants to bless us so much we don't have any more room for the blessings! What kinds of things have we been blessed with?

DISCOVERING PRAYER!

Snack time can be a great time to teach preschoolers about prayer. You can also take prayer requests, review previous prayer requests, and receive praise reports.

1. Does God like it when we pray?
2. Why is it important to pray?
3. Can we pray when we're happy?
4. Can we pray when we're sad?

LET'S CREATE!

Paper Plate Sheep
Supplies Needed: Thin paper plates, cotton balls, glue, black construction paper, and scissors.
- Give each child a paper plate folded in half.
- Use scissors to cut rectangles and circles out of the black construction paper for the legs and head of the sheep.
- Give each child two legs and a head. Help them glue the legs to the straight, folded edge of the paper plate and the head onto one of the rounded edges of the plate.
- Glue the halves of the paper plate together.
- Let the kids glue cotton balls on both sides of their sheep.

Psalm 23 Chain
Supplies Needed: Strips of colored construction paper, glue or stapler, marker.
- Before class, cut out strips of colored construction paper.
- On separate strips of paper write the following: "Psalm 23", "Green Pastures", "Quiet Waters", "Right Paths", Dark Valleys", "Rod and Staff", "Prepare a Table", "Cup Overflows" and, "Lord Forever". Make sure each child has one strip with each of the sayings on it.
- Show the kids how to make a chain by wrapping one of the strips into a circle and gluing it. Add another strip by threading it through the circle they just made and making another circle.
- Let the kids add blank strips to their chain if they want to.

Draw a Picture
Supplies Needed: Paper, crayons, pencils and/or markers.
- Give each child a piece of paper.
- Tell them to think about Psalm 23.
- Ask them to draw a picture of the psalm. Read the verses to them again if needed.

LESSON 4: THE 10 PLAGUES

Supplies Needed for this Lesson:

Green Balloons	A Jar	Red Food Coloring
Dot Stickers	Ping Pong Balls	Toy Locusts
Dry Cereal	Rice	Toy Flies
Toy Farm Animals	Toy Frogs	Blindfolds
Paper	Marker	Crayons
Scissors	Stencils	Glitter
Glue	Noodles	Misc. Craft Supplies
Costumes		

LET'S PLAY A GAME!

Individual Play

Capture the Frogs

Supplies Needed: Green balloons.

- Blow up several balloons before class.
- Have the kids try to keep the balloons from hitting the ground.
- If the challenge is too easy, add more balloons.

Multiple Play

Freeze Frog

Supplies Needed: None.

- This game is played like freeze tag.
- When the kids are tagged, instead of freezing, they have to hop around like a frog.
- They will continue like this until another player tags them and 'un-frogs' them.

MEMORY VERSE

Read the memory verse to the kids, showing them the hand motions to help them learn it. Have the kids repeat the verse with you a couple times while doing the hand motions.

I know - Point to your head.
The plans - Pretend to write on paper.
I have for you - Point to a friend.
Plans for good - Give a thumbs up.
And not for evil - Give a thumbs down.

> Copy and cut out the memory verse cards for this month so the kids can take them home to practice!

LET'S LEARN GOD'S WORD!

Teacher Preparation
Before class, choose one of the following Hands-On Activities for the kids to do while you read the story.

The 10 Plagues
Supplies Needed: A jar with a few drops of red food coloring on the bottom, cup of water, dot stickers, ping pong balls or marshmallows, toy locusts, dry cereal in a bowl, rice, toy flies, toy farm animals, toy frogs, blindfolds.

- As you go through the story, use the above items to demonstrate the plagues. Pour water into the jar with food coloring for blood. Place dot stickers on the kids for boils. Use ping pong balls for hail, rice for lice, dry cereal to show what it would feel like to walk on all those bugs, etc.
- Before beginning the lesson tell the kids God had a plan for the Hebrew people, but Pharaoh had a different plan. It wasn't the same as God's. God tried to convince Pharaoh that His plan was better than Pharaohs.
- **The verses for the last plague, death, have been included, but they are not covered in this lesson.**

Acting the Part
Supplies Needed: Costumes (optional).

- Assign children to be Moses, Aaron, Pharaoh and The Hebrew people. You can also assign children to be some of the different plagues like frogs or locusts.
- Read a small section of verses out of a children's Bible, then let the kids act out that scene in their own way.
- Continue until the whole story is read.

Read these verses out of a children's Bible while the kids do their hands-on activity. After reading the verses, engage the kids by asking questions about the text. On the next page are some questions to get you started.

Lesson Time Verses

Blood water - Exodus 7:14-18	Boils - Exodus 9:8-9
Frogs - Exodus 8:1-4	Hail - Exodus 9:13, 17-19
Lice - Exodus 8:16	Locusts - Exodus 10:3-6
Flies - Exodus 8:20-23	Darkness - Exodus 10:21-23
Sick Animals - Exodus 9:1-5	Death - Exodus 11:1, 4-5 (optional)

LET'S LEARN GOD'S WORD!

Discussion Questions

1. Why do you think Pharaoh wouldn't listen to Moses even after all God's miracles?
2. Do we ever have a hard time listening?
3. Do we get in trouble when we don't listen?
4. Would God have stopped the plagues if Pharaoh had listened to Him at the beginning?
5. Would God have stopped the plagues after He sent the second plague if Pharaoh had listened?
6. Can you imagine how smelly it would have been with all those dead frogs lying around?
7. Do you think God enjoyed seeing Pharaoh and his people go through all those things?
8. God knew His plan was better than Pharaoh's, but Pharaoh didn't want to listen. Are there ever times when we don't want to listen to our parents because we want something so bad?
9. Do you think we can learn from Pharaoh and remember that our parents and God want to keep us safe and have a plan for us?

DISCOVERING PRAYER!

Snack time can be a great time to teach preschoolers about prayer. You can also take prayer requests, review previous prayer requests, and receive praise reports.

1. What are some things we can talk about with God when we pray?
2. In our lesson, the Hebrew people prayed and asked God to help them. What kind of things can we pray and ask help for?

LET'S CREATE!

Helping Hand

Supplies Needed: Paper, marker, crayons, and scissors.
- Trace each child's hand on a piece of paper.
- Let the kids color the figure of their hands, then help the kids cut them out.
- While they are coloring, go around to each child with a marker and have them come up with one chore they can do for their parents. Write it and the child's name on the hand.

LET'S CREATE!

Draw a Picture
Supplies Needed: Paper, crayons.
- Have the kids draw a picture of something they learned today.

Make a Plan
Supplies Needed: Paper, crayons, stencils, glitter, glue, noodles, scraps of paper, and other miscellaneous craft supplies.
- Give each child a piece of paper and tell them they can make a picture of whatever they want, but they have to plan the picture first.
- Have the kids choose what items they're going to use. They can place those items on the paper to figure out where they want them before gluing them on.
- Once the kids are sure they have everything they need. Tell them they aren't allowed to change their plan and can only use the items chosen.
- Let the kids create their picture. As they create ask them if their plan is working the way they thought or if they wished they'd planned some more.
- Explain that we change our plans all the time, but God's plan for us is always the same.

LESSON 5: JOSEPH BECOMES A MIGHTY RULER

Supplies Needed for this Lesson:

Prizes	Two Coats	Four Big Boxes
Two Bins of Toys	Two Chairs	String
Spray Bottles	Paper Towels	A "Jail"
Scissors	Noodles	Paint
Paint Brushes	Paint Smocks	Crayons
Disposable Cups	Popsicle Sticks	Glue
Costumes	Green Construction Paper	

LET'S PLAY A GAME!

Individual Play
The Right Thing
Supplies Needed: Scenarios, prizes.
- Read a scenario to the kids and let them come up with things they should do in those situations. Give prizes to those who take part.

A friend comes to your house to play and they have some candy to share. Your mom tells you not to eat any candy before lunch, but mom isn't watching right now. What should you do?

You're in the backyard playing catch with your brother. He doesn't want to play anymore and you get mad. Your mom isn't feeling well and is taking a nap. What should you do?

A friend drops some money and they didn't notice. What should you do?

You're at church and a new girl is playing with your favorite toy. What should you do?

One of your friends is arguing with another child. The other child is saying some mean things to your friend. What should you do?

LET'S PLAY A GAME!

Multiple Play
Joseph Relay Race
Supplies Needed: Two coats, four boxes, two bins filled with any kind of toy, two chairs.
- Before class set up the race. Two coats on the ground, two boxes for a pit, two messes to clean up, two boxes for a jail, and two chairs for Pharaoh's throne.
- Split the kids into two teams and have them line up a few feet from the two coats.
- The first child in each team will run and put on the coat, then run back to the team.
- The next child will run to the 'pit', get in the box and stay there.
- The next child will run to the pit, help the child out and the two will run back.
- The next child will run to the mess and clean it up and run back to the team.
- The next child runs to the jail, gets in the box and stays there.
- The next child runs to the jail, gets the child out of jail, they both run back.
- The next child runs to Pharaoh's throne and sits down.
- The first team to finish wins. During the lesson explain how each station relates to the story.

MEMORY VERSE

Read the memory verse to the kids, showing them the hand motions to help them learn it. Have the kids repeat the verse with you a couple times while doing the hand motions.

I know - Point to your head.
The plans - Pretend to write on paper.
I have for you - Point to a friend.
Plans for good - Give a thumbs up.
And not for evil - Give a thumbs down.

> Copy and cut out the memory verse cards for this month so the kids can take them home to practice!

LET'S LEARN GOD'S WORD!

Teacher Preparation
Before class, choose one of the following Hands-On Activities for the kids to do while you read the story.

Joseph's Journey
Supplies Needed: A big box, string or yarn, spray bottles, paper towels, a "jail", and dress up clothes (optional).
- Before class set up three stations. A big box for the pit, Potiphar's house with spray bottles and paper towels so the kids can be slaves like Joseph was, and a jail cell. You can find more information about making a jail cell in the reference section on page 234.
- Tell the kids they're going to go on an adventure with Joseph today. Tell them God had a plan for Joseph and Joseph understood and trusted God. Even though the plan didn't work out the way Joseph thought it should, he still believed God would make His plan come to pass.
- As you read the story out of a children's Bible, have the kids march to each station. The kids can take turns getting into the pit, cleaning, and being in the jail.

Acting the Part
Supplies Needed: Costumes (optional).
- Assign parts to the children. You will need at least one brother, Joseph, Potiphar, Potiphar's wife, jail person who has a dream, and Pharaoh.
- Read a small section of the story out of a children's Bible and let the kids act it out in their own way.

Read these verses out of a children's Bible while the kids do their hands-on activity. After reading the verses, engage the kids by asking questions about the text. On the next page are some questions to get you started.

Lesson Time Verses
Genesis 37:3-5	**Genesis 39:1-4**	**Genesis 40:1-3, 8-13, 20-23**
Genesis 37:18-24	**Genesis 39:7-8, 14, 19-20**	
Genesis 41:1-4, 9-13, 14-15, 26-31, 33-36		

LET'S LEARN GOD'S WORD!

Discussion Questions

1. Joseph's brothers were jealous because Joseph was the favorite. They wanted to be the favorite like Joseph. Do you think we can love some of our family and friends in different ways?
2. It was a mean thing his brothers did to him, but God turned that bad thing into something good. Can it be hard to trust God when we feel like we're not getting our way?
3. How can we remind ourselves God has a plan for us when we aren't getting what we want?
4. Potiphar's wife wasn't nice either, she lied about Joseph, but God also used this bad thing to do something good. When we're mad or upset at a friend or our parents how can we make things good again?
5. One of the men Joseph was in jail with made a promise to do something for Joseph and then forgot. Have you ever forgotten to do something your parents told you to do?
6. What did the man do when he realized he'd forgotten about Joseph?
7. What can we do when we realize we've forgotten to do something our parents have asked us to do?

DISCOVERING PRAYER!

Snack time can be a great time to teach preschoolers about prayer. You can also take prayer requests, review previous prayer requests, and receive praise reports.

1. What kind of prayers are there?
2. What would be a sad or scared prayer?

LET'S CREATE!

God has a Plan for Me Egyptian Bracelet or Necklace
Supplies Needed: String, scissors, noodles, paint, paint brushes, crayons and copies of medallions from page 27.
- Give each child a medallion to color.
- Let the kids have a handful of noodles. Let them paint the noodles.
- Once the noodles are dry, give the kids a piece of string and let them put the noodles and medallion on it.
- Tie the string for the kids and let them wear their necklace/bracelet.

LET'S CREATE!

Joseph in a Pit Puppet
Supplies Needed: Plastic or paper cups, Popsicle sticks, crayons, glue, scissors, green construction paper.

- Give each child a small circle of paper and have them draw Joseph's face on it.
- Help them cut the picture out and glue it to a Popsicle stick.
- Have the kids cut out small pieces of green construction paper to glue around the top of the cup for grass.
- Cut a slit in the bottom of the cup to allow the Popsicle stick to go through.
- Show the children how to move the stick up and down to let Joseph in and out of the pit.

EGYPTIAN NECKLACE MEDALLIONS

God has a plan for me!

God has a plan for me!

God has a plan for me!

God has a plan for me!

God has a plan for me!

God has a plan for me!

JANUARY MEMORY VERSE CARDS

Jeremiah 29:11	Jeremiah 29:11
"I know the plans I have for you, plans for good and not evil."	"I know the plans I have for you, plans for good and not evil."

Jeremiah 29:11	Jeremiah 29:11
"I know the plans I have for you, plans for good and not evil."	"I know the plans I have for you, plans for good and not evil."

Jeremiah 29:1	Jeremiah 29:11
"I know the plans I have for you, plans for good and not evil."	"I know the plans I have for you, plans for good and not evil."

Jeremiah 29:11	Jeremiah 29:11
"I know the plans I have for you, plans for good and not evil."	"I know the plans I have for you, plans for good and not evil."

FEBRUARY
GOD LOVES YOU!

OVERVIEW

In these lessons, the children will learn what love looks like, how God and their parents love them, and how they can love others. **This will also include ideas for service projects the kids can do.**

Memory Verse

1 John 5:3

"Loving God means obeying His commands."

Hand Motions

Loving God
Cross hands over chest.

Means obeying
March in place.

His
Point up.

Commands
Pretend to write on paper.

LESSON 1: What is Love? 1 Corinthians 13
God defined love for us in 1 Corinthians 13. This lesson will explore those definitions and help the children understand what each one means.

LESSON 2: The 10 Commandments
The 10 Commandments provides us with a simple list of rules to follow. This lesson will explore the connection between rules and love. The kids will learn that even though parents may set a lot of rules, they do it because they love us and God is the same way.

LESSON 3: Jesus Calls the Children
This story is a classic one for preschoolers. This lesson will explore the idea that even when children feel left out or unimportant Jesus is always there for them.

LESSON 4: Loving Others
God wants us to love others. This lesson is not based on a specific scripture. Instead, it explores different ways the children can serve their community. **This may require a few weeks of preparation in advance if you want the kids to collect items to give to a charity or organization.**

LESSON 5: The Good Samaritan
In the story of the Good Samaritan, Jesus is answering the question "Who is my neighbor?". This lesson will explore that question with the kids on their level and in their life situations.

LESSON 1: WHAT IS LOVE? 1 CORINTHIANS 13

Supplies Needed for this Lesson:

Marker	Pictures of the Kids	Children's Bible
Candy	Colored Construction Paper	Glue
Tape	Ribbon or Yarn	Colored Cardstock
Paper Plates	Hole Punch	Scissors

LET'S PLAY A GAME!

Individual Play

My Friends Match
Supplies Needed: Pictures of each child printed twice, marker.
- Before class, print out the pictures and with a marker, write on the back "God Loves…"
- Mix up the pictures and place them face down on the table.
- Let the kids take turns flipping over two of the pictures.
- For each picture they turn over have them say "God Loves…" and the name of the person in the picture.
- When a match is made, move the cards to the side.
- Play until all matches have been made.

Multiple Play

God's Word – Keep It!
Supplies Needed: Children's Bible.
- Play this game like "Hot Potato".
- Have the kids sit in a circle.
- Turn the music on and have the kids pass the Bible around.
- When the music stops, have the child holding the Bible shout "I Have God's Love Letter!".

MEMORY VERSE

Read the memory verse to the kids, showing them the hand motions to help them learn it. Have the kids repeat the verse with you a couple times while doing the hand motions.

Loving God – Cross hands over chest.
Means obeying – March in place.
His – Point up.
Commands – Pretend to write on paper.

> Copy and cut out the memory verse cards for this month so the kids can take them home to practice!

LET'S LEARN GOD'S WORD!

Teacher Preparation
Before class, choose one of the following Hands-On Activities for the kids to do while you read the story.

Acting in Love
Supplies Needed: Scenarios.
- Have the kids act out each scene.
- Ask the kids to point out who showed loved and who didn't.

> Some kids are at the park playing tag. A little girl asks if she can play, but they won't let her. The girl starts to cry. Two kids playing on the swings ask her what's wrong. When she tells them, the two kids decide to start their own game of tag with the little girl.
>
> Mom is making dinner and asks her two kids to go play quietly in their room until dinner is ready. One child obeys, but the other complains and argues.
>
> Two friends are playing with blocks in the living room. Dad comes in and tells the children to start cleaning up. The kids say they will, but after dad leaves the room, they keep playing and don't pick up at all. Five minutes later dad comes back and finds they haven't cleaned anything up. He is mad at them for not doing what they said they would do. The kids start to pick up the toys and apologize to dad for not doing it earlier.
>
> A little boy is at his Grandma's house with his parents because Grandma is sick. The child decides to find some books and tell stories to his grandma. He also gets her a drink of water and helps his parents carry in some soup for her to eat.

LET'S LEARN GOD'S WORD!

Practicing Love
Supplies Needed: Candy.
- Read through 1 Corinthians 13:4-7, stopping after each characteristic of love.
- Give an example to the kids using candy.
- **Love is patient**: Give each child a piece of candy and tell them they can't eat it until the lesson is over. They are practicing being patient.
- **Love is kind:** Ask the kids what it means to be kind. Ask if anyone wants to be kind by giving you their piece of candy. If any of them do, thank them.
- **Love is not jealous:** Give a second piece of candy to those who didn't give you theirs. Ask the others how they feel about not getting another piece of candy.
- **Love does not brag:** If any children have made bragging remarks point it out.
- **Love is not rude:** Ask the kids if they know what it means to be rude. As they answer, reach over and take someone's candy. Ask if that was rude of you.
- **Love is not selfish:** Ask the kids who have two candies, to give one of their candies to someone who doesn't have any. Ask them if it was hard to give the candy away. Explain that keeping all the candy to themselves is being selfish, but sharing is not.
- **Love does not anger easily:** Ask the kids if any of them have felt angry during the lesson. Explain that God wants us to try to not get angry.
- **Love does not remember wrongs done against it:** Remind the kids of the stolen candy. Explain that God doesn't want us to hold onto those angry feelings, but wants us to forgive people.
- **Love is not happy when others do wrong, but is always happy with the truth:** Ask the kids if it was wrong of you to take the child's candy. Ask if they should join someone doing wrong, or try to do the right thing. Explain that God doesn't want us to do things that are wrong.
- **Love never gives up on people, never stops trusting, never loses hope and never quits:** Hand out candy so each child has two pieces. Tell the kids they can now eat their candy and they've done a great job being patient. Have the kids come up with ways they can show love to people at home.

Read these verses out of a children's Bible while the kids do their hands-on activity. After reading the verses, engage the kids by asking questions about the text. On the next page are some questions to get you started.

Lesson Time Verses
1 Corinthians 13:4-7

LET'S LEARN GOD'S WORD!

Discussion Questions

1. Did you learn anything new about what it means to love people?
2. How can we love our mom's and dad's more?
3. Do you think it can be hard to love people sometimes?
4. Can you name a time when your parents were kind to you?
5. Can you name a time when your parents were patient with you?

DISCOVERING PRAYER!

Snack time can be a great time to teach preschoolers about prayer. You can also take prayer requests, review previous prayer requests, and receive praise reports.

1. Who can we pray for?
2. How can we pray when we've done something wrong?

LET'S CREATE!

Showing God's Love Paper Heart Chains
Supplies Needed: Colored construction paper, scissors, glue, tape, marker, ribbon or yarn.
- Before class cut out several hearts of the same size from different colored paper.
- Fold the hearts in half and cut out the middle section. Put the small, whole hearts in a scrap pile for other projects or throw away. This project will use the hearts with the hole in the middle.
- Have each child pick out seven hearts for themselves.
- Have the kids come up with ways they can show love to people this week and write down their ideas on the hearts. They'll have one heart for each day of the week.
- Help the kids cut through one side of their hearts.
- Have the kids link the hearts together and glue or tape the cuts closed again to make a paper chain.
- Give each child a piece of ribbon or yarn to tie around one of the hearts so they can hang it up.
- Explain to the kids that they can tear one heart off each time they show God's love to another person.

LET'S CREATE!

What is Love Wreath

Supplies Needed: Colored cardstock, scissors, glue, paper plates, yarn or ribbon, hole punch.

- Before class cut out hearts from cardstock. Each child will need nine hearts.
- Write each description of love from 1 Corinthians 13 on the hearts and make sure each child gets one of each.
- Give each child a paper plate to decorate with crayons.
- When they finish decorating their plates help the children glue one heart to the middle of their plate. Glue the other hearts around the edge of the plate.
- Use a hole punch to put a hole in the plate. Tie on a ribbon or piece of yarn.

LESSON 2: THE 10 COMMANDMENTS

Supplies Needed for this Lesson:

Green & Red Paper	Paint	Paint Smocks	Tape
Paint Brushes	Crayons	Scissors	String
Colored Cardstock	Brads	Small Envelopes	Paper
Paper Plates			

LET'S PLAY A GAME!

Individual Play

Follow the Leader

Supplies Needed: None.

- Have the kids get in a line behind you. Have them follow you around the room.
- Make them do different actions. (hop, skip, jump etc.)

Multiple Play

Obey the Rules

Supplies Needed: One green and one red piece of paper, paper plates.

- Give each child a paper plate and tell them it is their steering wheel.
- Tell the kids they can drive around as much as they like, but they can't crash into each other or the wall, or any furniture.
- They also have to obey the traffic lights. Show them the papers, green means "GO" red means "STOP".
- Let the kids run around the room. Every now and then hold up the red paper. If the kids don't stop, tell them they have to sit down for 15 seconds before they can go again.

MEMORY VERSE

Read the memory verse to the kids, showing them the hand motions to help them learn it. Have the kids repeat the verse with you a couple times while doing the hand motions.

Loving God – Cross hands over chest.
Means obeying – March in place.
His – Point up.
Commands – Pretend to write on paper.

> Copy and cut out the memory verse cards for this month so the kids can take them home to practice!

LET'S LEARN GOD'S WORD!

Teacher Preparation
Before class, choose one of the following Hands-On Activities for the kids to do while you read the story.

Commandments Review Game
Supplies Needed: None.
- Have the kids stand in a line.
- Tell the kids to take a step forward, leap, skip once etc., if they've ever obeyed the first commandment.
- Repeat with the remaining commandments.
- When you've gone through all the commandments, show the kids how far they came and explain that it's not hard to follow God's rules.

Paint a Mural
Supplies Needed: Paint, paper, paint smocks, water, brushes and tape.
- Tape butcher paper to the wall, or give each child an individual piece of paper and tape them together later.
- As you read through the Bible verses, have the kids paint pictures of what it looks like to obey the 10 commandments.

Read these verses out of a children's Bible while the kids do their hands-on activity. After reading the verses, engage the kids by asking questions about the text. Below are some questions to get you started.

Lesson Time Verses
Exodus 20:1-3	Exodus 20:13
Exodus 20:4	Exodus 20:14
Exodus 20:7	Exodus 20:15
Exodus 20:8-11	Exodus 20:16
Exodus 20:12	Exodus 20:17

Discussion Questions
1. What rules do you have to follow at home? Do you like having rules?
2. What are your least favorite rules?
3. What would you do if there were no rules?
4. Why do you think parents give us rules?
5. Who else gives us rules? What are some of the rules in our classroom?
6. What do you think it means to worship something?
7. What is a day of rest or Sabbath? When do you take a day of rest?
8. What do you think about the rule about respecting and honoring your parents?
9. Do you think that means you need to obey their rules?

DISCOVERING PRAYER

Snack time can be a great time to teach preschoolers about prayer. You can also take prayer requests, review previous prayer requests, and receive praise reports.

1. When we pray do we always have to ask God for something?
2. What are some things we can thank God for today?

LET'S CREATE!

10 Commandments Train
Supplies Needed: Copies of train pieces from pages 38 and 39, crayons, scissors, string, or brads.
- Give each child one train piece to color.
- Help them cut the pieces out.
- Let the kids help put the train together by gluing the train onto a long piece of string or by connecting the pieces with brads.
- Put the train up on the classroom wall.

10 Commandments Hearts
Supplies Needed: Colored cardstock, scissors, crayons, small envelopes.
- Before class cut out several hearts from cardstock so each child can have one whole heart. Make several more hearts and cut off the rounded part so you have three separate pieces. Throw the triangle part away or put it in a scrap paper pile for other crafts.
- On each rounded piece of heart, write one of the 10 commandments. So each child will have one whole heart and 10 rounded pieces of a heart.
- On the whole heart write "God Loves Us".
- Explain that each heart piece has one of God's rules on it.
- Have the kids color their heart pieces.
- Show the kids how they can stack the rounded heart pieces on top of their whole heart. It will show them God's commandments.
- Give each child an envelope with their name on it.
- Let them decorate their envelope and put their heart and heart pieces inside for safe keeping.

10 COMMANDMENTS TRAIN

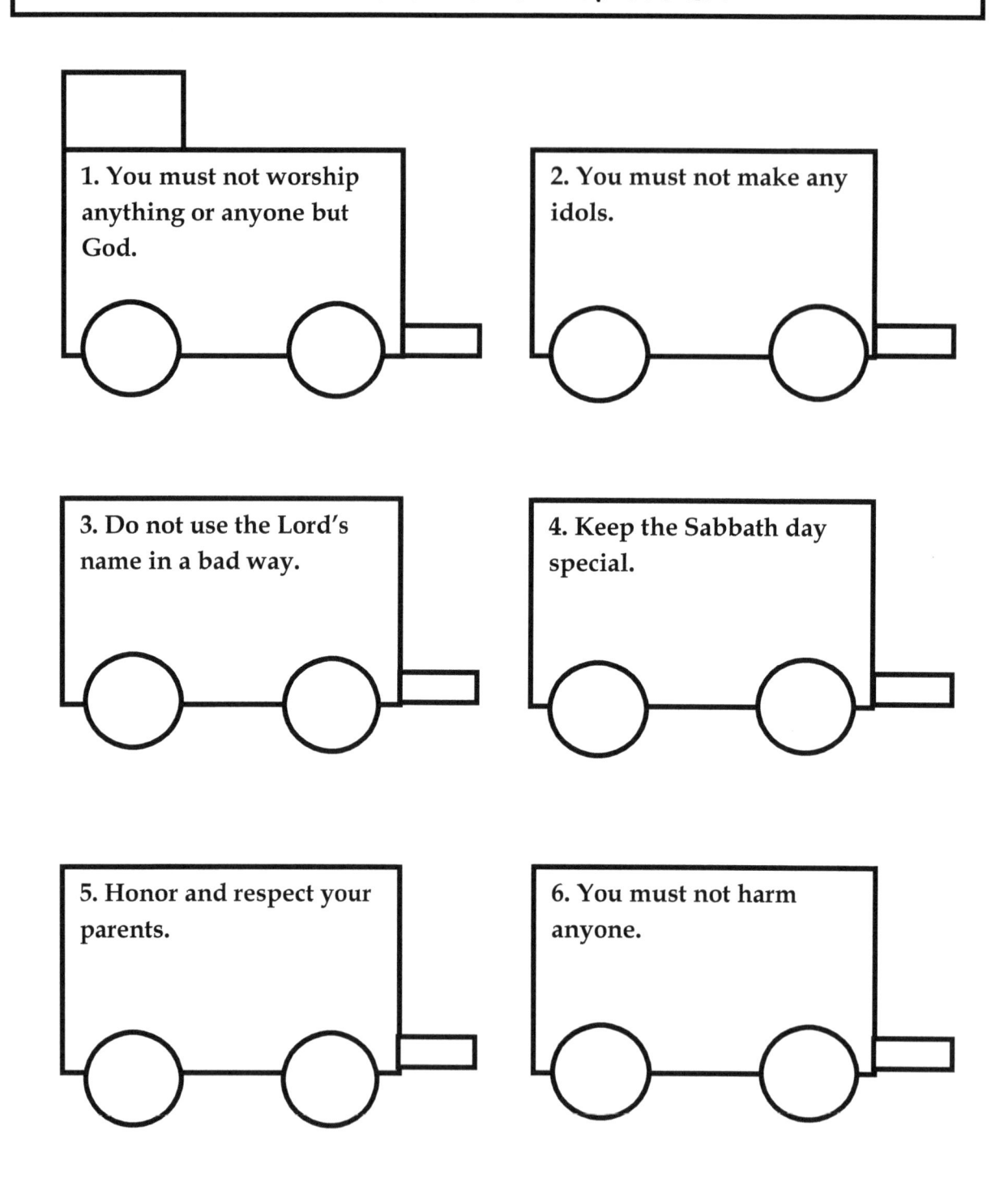

1. You must not worship anything or anyone but God.

2. You must not make any idols.

3. Do not use the Lord's name in a bad way.

4. Keep the Sabbath day special.

5. Honor and respect your parents.

6. You must not harm anyone.

10 COMMANDMENTS TRAIN

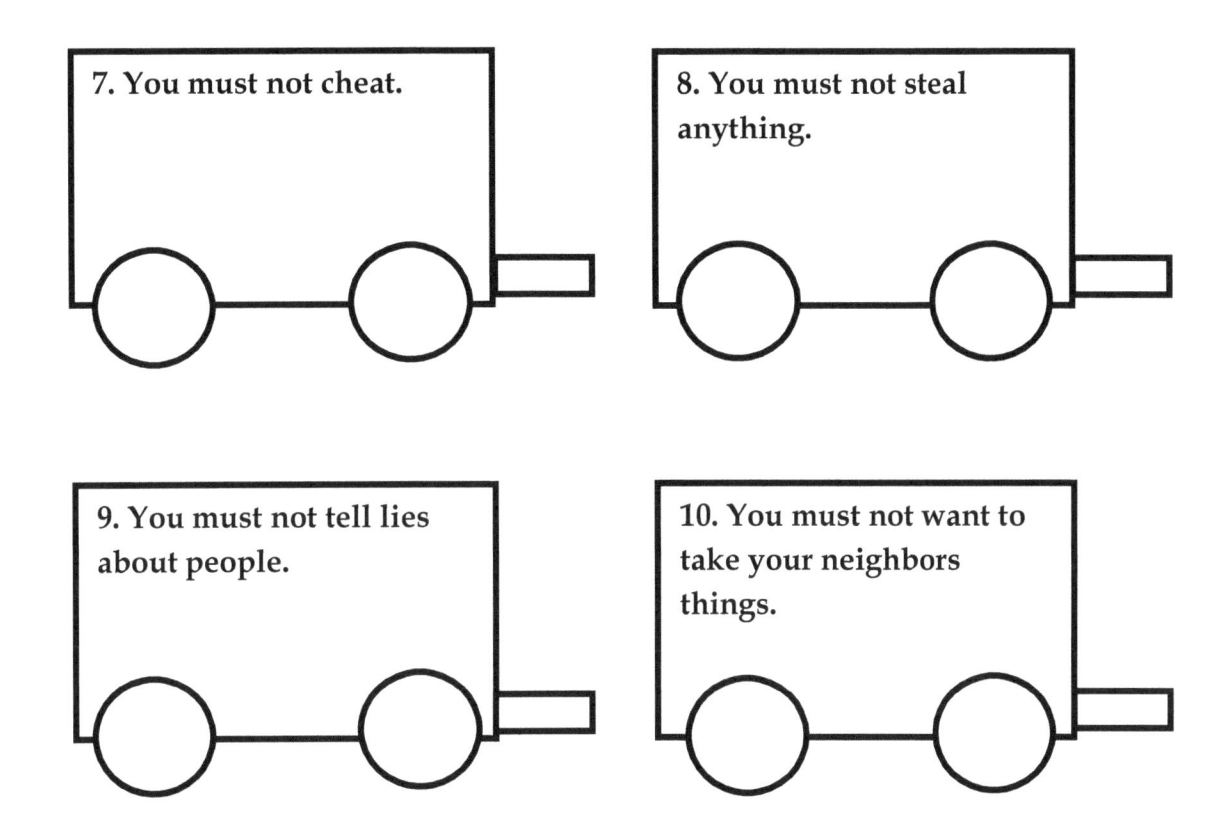

7. You must not cheat.

8. You must not steal anything.

9. You must not tell lies about people.

10. You must not want to take your neighbors things.

LESSON 3: JESUS CALLS THE CHILDREN

Supplies Needed for this Lesson:

Male Toy Figurine	Pictures of the Kids	Glue
Scissors	Popsicle Sticks	String
Stickers	Marker	Paint
Paint Brushes	Paint Smocks	Crayons
Hole Punch	Yarn	Costumes
Random Toys		

LET'S PLAY A GAME!

Individual Play

Find Jesus
Supplies Needed: Small, male toy figurine.
- Show the figure to the kids and tell them it is Jesus and He is going off to teach some adults.
- Have all the kids close their eyes, then hide the figure of Jesus.
- Have the kids try to find Jesus.
- Continue play until allotted time for games is up.

Multiple Play

Disciples Block the Children
Supplies Needed: None.
- Play this game like "Red Rover".
- Have several kids link arms together. They are the disciples.
- Have the rest of the kids line up on the other side of the room.
- Explain that they are trying to go see Jesus, but they have to get through the disciples.
- Have one child at a time, try to break through the disciples. If they fail, have all the kids shout "Don't keep the kids from me!".
- Then the disciples will let the child through.
- If the child breaks through, have the child shout "I made it to Jesus!".
- Once a child has tried to break through, have them join the disciples. Send one of the disciples to the other side of the room until all children have taken a turn.

MEMORY VERSE

Read the memory verse to the kids, showing them the hand motions to help them learn it. Have the kids repeat the verse with you a couple times while doing the hand motions.

Loving God – Cross hands over chest.
Means obeying – March in place.
His – Point up.
Commands – Pretend to write on paper.

> Copy and cut out the memory verse cards for this month so the kids can take them home to practice!

LET'S LEARN GOD'S WORD!

Teacher Preparation
Before class, choose one of the following Hands-On Activities for the kids to do while you read the story.

Acting the Part
Supplies Needed: Costumes (optional).
- Let the kids act out the story while you tell it.
- Have some of the kids act as parents, some as disciples, one as Jesus and the rest as children.

A Toy's Tale
Supplies Needed: Toys from around the room.
- Let the kids pick out animals or dolls from around the room.
- Let the kids act out the scenes with the toys.

Read these verses out of a children's Bible while the kids do their hands-on activity. After reading the verses, engage the kids by asking questions about the text. Below are some questions to get you started.

Lesson Time Verses
Mark 10:13-16

Discussion Questions

1. Do you feel loved ALL the time, or are there times when you don't feel loved? Can you name some of those times?
2. Why do you think the disciples thought Jesus wouldn't want to see the children?
3. Do you ever feel like someone has forgotten about you? How did it make you feel?
4. Jesus knows what it's like to feel forgotten so He never forgets about anyone. What can we do to make sure others don't feel forgotten by us?

DISCOVERING PRAYER

Snack time can be a great time to teach preschoolers about prayer. You can also take prayer requests, review previous prayer requests, and receive praise reports.

1. Should you pray when you feel forgotten?
2. Can you think of someone you can be extra nice to this week?
3. If you see someone crying, what can you do to help them?

LET'S CREATE!

Jesus Loves Me Craft
Supplies Needed: Pictures of each child printed out, glue, scissors, Popsicle sticks, string, stickers, paint, paint smocks, paint brushes, water, and marker.
- Give each child four Popsicle sticks.
- Help them glue the sticks into a square.
- Let the kids decorate their sticks.
- Help the kids glue their picture to the back of the frame once their frames are dry.
- Give each child a piece of string and help them glue the ends to the back of their frame so they can hang their picture.
- Before each child leaves write "Jesus Loves Me" on the bottom of the frame.

Jesus Loves You Bookmarks
Supplies Needed: Copies of bookmarks from page 43, crayons, scissors, hole punch, yarn.
- Give each child a page of bookmarks to color.
- Tell the kids to color them as beautiful as they can because they are going to give the bookmarks to people who need to know God loves them.
- When the kids finish coloring, help them cut the bookmarks out.
- Punch a hole in the top of each bookmark and let the kids choose a color of yarn to tie onto their bookmarks.

JESUS LOVES ME BOOKMARKS

Jesus Loves Me!

Jesus Loves Me!

LESSON 4: LOVING OTHERS

Supplies Needed for this Lesson:

Masking Tape	Butcher Paper	Paint	Tape
Paint Smocks	Paint Brushes	Crayons	Stickers
Flower Pots	Potting Soil	Flowers	Paper
Construction Paper	Scissors	Glue	Noodles
String	Yarn	Beads	Fabric Scraps
Misc. Craft Supplies			

LET'S PLAY A GAME!

Individual Play

Who does Jesus Love?

Supplies Needed: Masking tape.

- Before class, create a large heart on the floor with masking tape.
- Have the kids sit on the outside of the heart.
- Tell the kids we're going to find out who Jesus loves.
- When they hear their name called, they're going to jump into the heart.
- Have all the kids say "Who does Jesus love?".
- Say one of their names and have them jump into the heart.
- Have all the kids say "Jesus loves ____".
- When all the kids are in the heart, do the same for the teachers.
- When everyone is in the heart have the kids shout "Who does Jesus love? Jesus loves everyone!"

Multiple Play

Help Me Paint a Picture

Supplies Needed: Butcher paper, paint, water, tape, paint smocks, brushes.

- Cut off enough butcher paper so two kids can easily paint on one piece together.
- Divide the kids into groups of two and give each group a picture to paint: sun, flower, clouds etc.
- The children need to work together and practice loving one another as they paint.
- The kids are drawing one picture, not two, so both have to have a part in painting the picture.
- Each child can do half of the painting, or one can do a certain part and the other can do another part, but they have to make only one picture.
- Remind them to be patient and kind to one another and to use nice words.
- When they're done, praise them for working together and showing love to each other.

MEMORY VERSE

Read the memory verse to the kids, showing them the hand motions to help them learn it. Have the kids repeat the verse with you a couple times, doing the hand motions.

Loving God – Cross hands over chest.
Means obeying – March in place.
His – Point up.
Commands – Pretend to write on paper.

> Copy and cut out the memory verse cards for this month so the kids can take them home to practice!

LET'S LEARN GOD'S WORD!

> ### Teacher Preparation
> Before class, choose one of the following Hands-On Activities for the kids to do while you read the story.

Planting for Seniors
Supplies Needed: Pots, dirt, flowers, water.
- Have the kids decorate flower pots.
- Help them plant flowers into the pots.
- Tell the kids the plants will be going to a senior center to cheer up some people who might be lonely.
- You can also send the pot home with a flyer that explains the service project and have the families deliver the flowers themselves. A flyer has been made for you in the reference section on pages 236 and 237.
- If you are able to, you can also schedule a time for the kids to meet at a specific senior center and have them hand the plants out.

Military Cards
Supplies Needed: Paper, crayons, stickers.
- Have the kids create cards for people in the military or military families. They can be for service members and families in your church. You can also send them to an organization who will deliver the cards to military personnel. You can find some of the organizations in the reference section in this book on pages 238 and 239.

LET'S LEARN GOD'S WORD!

Discussion Questions

1. When people receive our donations, how do you think it will make them feel?
2. Was it a lot of work putting these together?
3. Does it make you feel good knowing how much work you put in to making people feel loved?
4. What are some things we can do to help people when we're at home?
5. What other kinds of service projects would you like to do here at church?
6. Do you remember any of our lessons about God loving people?
7. What are some of the things you remember?
8. Did we do any of those things today with our service project?
9. Do you think it's fun to serve others? Why?

DISCOVERING PRAYER

Snack time can be a great time to teach preschoolers about prayer. You can also take prayer requests, review previous prayer requests, and receive praise reports.

1. Do you think it's possible to pray for people you've never met?
2. What can we pray for the people who will be getting our donations?

LET'S CREATE!

Love Cards
Supplies Needed: Construction paper, scissors, glue, crayons, paint, stickers, noodles, string, yarn, fabric scraps and other miscellaneous craft supplies.
- Put the craft supplies on the table and let the kids create cards for people they love.
- Help the kids glue and cut.

Kindness Necklace
Supplies Needed: String, beads.
- Tell the kids they're going to make a kindness necklace to give to someone they love.
- Give each child a piece of string with a knot in one end.
- Show the kids how to put the beads on the string and let the kids create necklaces. When they're done, help them tie the ends together.

LESSON 5: THE GOOD SAMARITAN

Supplies Needed for this Lesson:

Building Blocks	Toy Figurines	Band-Aids	Play-Doh
Cookie Cutters	Paper	Paint Smocks	Paint
Envelopes	Gauze	Q-Tips	Scissors
Crayons	Costumes	Small Cups	Stickers

LET'S PLAY A GAME!

Individual Play

Be a Good Samaritan

Supplies Needed: Building blocks, toy figurines.

- Place several toy figurines on tables or chairs. The toys are injured people who need to be rescued.
- Have the kids build rescue towers out of blocks to save the people.

Multiple Play

The Good Samaritan Game

Supplies Needed: Band-Aids, small cups of water.

- Divide the kids into groups of four.
- Give each group two Band-Aids.
- Have the kids decide who in their group will be the injured person.
- Tell the kids they are going to race to see who can help the injured person first.
- When you say "Go", have the kids run to their injured person, put the two Band-Aids on them and give them a drink of water.
- The first team to finish wins.
- When the game is over, talk about how it felt to help someone and praise them for working together as a team.

MEMORY VERSE

Read the memory verse to the kids, showing them the hand motions to help them learn it. Have the kids repeat the verse with you a couple times while doing the hand motions.

Loving God – Cross hands over chest.
Means obeying – March in place.
His – Point up.
Commands – Pretend to write on paper.

> Copy and cut out the memory verse cards for this month so the kids can take them home to practice

LET'S LEARN GOD'S WORD!

Teacher Preparation
Before class, choose one of the following Hands-On Activities for the kids to do while you read the story.

Acting the Part
Supplies Needed: Costumes (optional).
- Have kids act out the different scenes as you read the story.
- Parts needed are: Samaritan, two people who pass by, the wounded man, hotel clerk, muggers.

A Play-Doh Scene
Supplies Needed: Play-Doh, cookie cutters.
- Have the kids create the characters from the story out of Play-Doh as you tell the story.

Read these verses out of a children's Bible while the kids do their hands-on activity. After reading the verses, engage the kids by asking questions about the text. Below are some questions to get you started.

Lesson Time Verses
Luke 10:30
Luke 10:31-32
Luke 10:33-34
Luke 10:35

Discussion Questions

1. Does it feel better to help someone who is hurting or to ignore them?
2. If you see a child on the playground fall and hurt themselves what can you do to help?
3. Why do you think two of the people who passed the hurt man in our story, kept walking and didn't help?
4. The Good Samaritan didn't just help the hurt man, he also paid for a hotel room for him so he could rest and get better. He went above and beyond what he needed to do. What extra things can we do for our parents, brothers, sisters, or friends?
5. Do any of your parents keep first aid kits on hand? What kind of things do you put into a first aid kit?

DISCOVERING PRAYER

Snack time can be a great time to teach preschoolers about prayer. You can also take prayer requests, review previous prayer requests, and receive praise reports.

1. Do you always have to be quiet when you're praying?
2. What kinds of things can we pray about for our brothers, sisters and friends?

LET'S CREATE!

Finger Paint Flowers
Supplies Needed: Paper, paint, paint smocks.
- Give each child a piece of paper.
- Tell the kids to paint pictures of flowers with their finger.
- Let the paint dry.
- Tell the kids they can give their picture to someone who looks sad and needs cheering up.

First Aid Kit
Supplies Needed: Envelopes, Band-Aids, Q-tips, gauze, crayons, and stickers.
- Give each child an envelope and tell them they are going to create a first aid kit so they can be a Good Samaritan when they see someone get hurt.
- Let the kids decorate their envelopes.
- Then let them take a couple Band-Aids, Q-tips and some Gauze to put in their envelopes.

FEBRUARY MEMORY VERSE CARDS

1 John 5:3 "Loving God means obeying His commands."	1 John 5:3 "Loving God means obeying His commands."
1 John 5:3 "Loving God means obeying His commands."	1 John 5:3 "Loving God means obeying His commands."
1 John 5:3 "Loving God means obeying His commands."	1 John 5:3 "Loving God means obeying His commands."
1 John 5:3 "Loving God means obeying His commands."	1 John 5:3 "Loving God means obeying His commands."

MARCH
GOD SAVED YOU!

OVERVIEW

The holiday of Easter is all about how God rescued us from sin. These lessons will follow Jesus in the days leading up to Resurrection Sunday. They will also give a little bit of background on why Jesus had to die on the cross. **Because Easter doesn't land in the same month each year, feel free to use these lessons in April instead of March.**

Memory Verse

Romans 10:13

"Anyone who calls on the name of the Lord will be saved."

Hand Motions

Anyone
Wave your hand in front of you.

Who calls on the name
Put your hands up to you mouth as if shouting.

Of the Lord
Point up.

Will be saved
Cross your hands over each other as though they're handcuffed, then pull them apart.

LESSON 1: Adam & Eve: The First Sin
God never intended us to be sick, or broken in spirit. He never meant for there to be bad things. This lesson will explore the first sin, how our relationship with God was injured by that sin and God's plan to fix it.

LESSON 2: Palm Sunday
The day Jesus rode into the city on the back of a donkey was a day of celebration. People were celebrating all the things Jesus had done for them. This lesson will be a party for Jesus.

LESSON 3: The Last Supper
Three major things happen at the last supper. Jesus washes his follower's feet, He explains the communion elements and tells who is going to betray him. This lesson will explore those three themes with an emphasis on the washing of the feet and the communion elements.

LESSON 4: Jesus' Death and Resurrection
The death of Jesus was a horrific event. This lesson will explore the reasons why Jesus had to die for us and doesn't focus so much on the gore and blood. It will end on the wonderfully happy note that Jesus came back to life and rescued us from sin.

LESSON 5: What Jesus did While in the Grave
This lesson will be a review of what Jesus did for us and why. The kids will also celebrate all that Jesus has done for us.

LESSON 1: ADAM & EVE: THE FIRST SIN

Supplies Needed for this Lesson:

Crayons	Colored Paper	Glue	Googly Eyes
Finger Paint	Toilet Paper Rolls	Pipe Cleaner	Fruit Stickers
Costumes	Paper	Construction Paper	

LET'S PLAY A GAME!

Individual Play

God Says
Supplies Needed: None.
- Play this game like "Simon Says".
- Tell the kids that when you say "God says…" and then you give a command such as "Rub your belly." The kids need to obey the command.
- Remind them to listen carefully. If a child obeys a command given without saying "God says", they will be out.
- When the game is over, explain that it's important that we learn to know God's commands so we can follow His instructions.

Multiple Play

Hide & Seek
Supplies Needed: None.
- Have the kids play a game of hide and seek.
- Tell the kids they are Adam and Eve and they are hiding from God.
- Select one child to be 'God' who is looking for Adam and Eve.

MEMORY VERSE

Read the memory verse to the kids, showing them the hand motions to help them learn it. Have the kids repeat the verse with you a couple times while doing the hand motions.

Anyone – Wave your hand in front of you.
Who calls on the name – Put your hands up to your mouth as if shouting.
Of the Lord – Point up.
Will be saved – Cross your hands over each other as though they're handcuffed, then pull them apart.

> Copy and cut out the memory verse cards for this month so the kids can take them home to practice!

LET'S LEARN GOD'S WORD!

Teacher Preparation
Before class, choose one of the following Hands-On Activities for the kids to do while you read the story.

Acting the Part
Supplies Needed: Costumes (optional).
- Assign parts to the kids so they can act out the story.
- If there are a lot of kids, break them up into groups and let each group act out the story.
- Parts needed for this story: Snake (devil), Jesus, Adam, and Eve.

Draw Me a Picture
Supplies Needed: Crayons, markers or pencils, paper.
- Give each child a piece of paper.
- Have them draw pictures of animals or people they hear about in the story as you read it to them.

Read these verses out of a children's Bible while the kids do their hands-on activity. After reading the verses, engage the kids by asking questions about the text. Below are some questions to get you started.

Lesson Time Verses
Genesis 3:1-3
Genesis 3:4-6
Genesis 3:7-9
Genesis 3:10-13

Discussion Questions
1. What was the first sin?
2. Do you ever have trouble obeying your parents?
3. Because of the first sin, every person that's born has sin in them, but with Jesus' help we can choose not to sin. Are there some things we can make better choices about this week?
4. Do you know what Jesus did to take care of sin?
5. Did you know, when Jesus died to take care of your sin, He sent the Holy Spirit to live inside of you and His job is to help you not sin? It's called the gift of salvation. Do any of you want to pray and receive the gift of salvation?

DISCOVERING PRAYER

Snack time can be a great time to teach preschoolers about prayer. You can also take prayer requests, review previous prayer requests, and receive praise reports.

1. Do you think we should thank Jesus for the gift of salvation?
2. Do you think it's ok to pray and not ask for anything, but just thank God for what He's already done for us?
3. What are some things we can thank God for today?

LET'S CREATE!

Paper Chain Snake
Supplies Needed: Strips of different colored paper, glue, googly eyes, red paper cut out to look like a snake tongue.
- Let the kids glue strips of paper into chains, as long as they want.
- On one end, help the kids glue on two googly eyes and a snake tongue.

Finger Paint Tree
Supplies Needed: Plain paper, finger paint.
- Give each child a piece of paper and ask them to create a tree with the finger paints.
- Have the kids paint fruit, Adam and Eve, the snake and Jesus too if they want.

Tree Craft
Supplies Needed: Toilet paper rolls, pipe cleaner, construction paper, apple or other fruit stickers.
- Before class, cut out the shape of a tree top out of green construction paper.
- Cut two small slits in the top of each toilet paper roll.
- Have the kids wrap pipe cleaner around the toilet paper roll like a snake
- Have the kids put fruit stickers on their tree top.
- Have the kids place the tree top into the slits on the toilet paper roll.

LESSON 2: PALM SUNDAY

Supplies Needed for this Lesson:

Long Stick
Special Snack
Paint Brushes
Plastic Eggs
Costumes
Party Music
Party Hats
Small Rocks
Beans or Rice
Building Blocks
Old Coats, Blankets etc.
Paint Smocks
Colored Electric Tape
Juice
Paint
Tape
Stickers

LET'S PLAY A GAME!

Individual Play

Limbo
Supplies Needed: Stick, music.
- Have the kids line up. Turn the music on, and have the kids walk under the stick.
- After each child has gone under once, lower the stick.
- Encourage the kids to cheer each other on.
- When the game is over, praise the kids for encouraging each other.

Multiple Play

Create a Path for Jesus
Supplies Needed: Building blocks.
- Divide the kids into two teams. Give each team a certain number of blocks to use. Depending on your supply, this may be a lot, or not very many.
- Tell the kids they need to work together to build a path for Jesus. They also need to make sure there is enough room for all the crowds of people.
- Tell the teams they only have three minutes to build their path.
- The team who uses the most, or all their blocks in a creative way, wins.

MEMORY VERSE

Read the memory verse to the kids, showing them the hand motions to help them learn it. Have the kids repeat the verse with you a couple times while doing the hand motions.

Anyone – Wave your hand in front of you.
Who calls on the name – Put your hands up to your mouth as if shouting.
Of the Lord – Point up.
Will be saved – Cross your hands over each other as though they're handcuffed, then pull them apart.

> Copy and cut out the memory verse cards for this month so the kids can take them home to practice!

LET'S LEARN GOD'S WORD!

Teacher Preparation
Before class, choose one of the following Hands-On Activities for the kids to do while you read the story.

Acting the Part
Supplies Needed: Costumes (optional).
- Have the kids act out the story as you read it.

Palm Party
Supplies Needed: Juice, special snack, party hats, party music, items to use as palm leaves, or coats. (Blankets, towels etc.)
- Tell the kids that Palm Sunday was the day everyone celebrated Jesus because of all the amazing miracles he had performed.
- Tell the kids we are going to have a party to celebrate all of the amazing things Jesus has done for us.
- Turn the music on and let the kids dance around.
- Every now and then ask the kids what amazing things Jesus has done for them.
- When they give an answer, have everyone shout "Praise Jesus!"
- After a little while, hand out the special snack.
- Have everyone wait to eat until all the snacks are passed out.
- After you pass out snacks, tell them the story of Palm Sunday.
- You can include the prayer lesson at the end of this as well.

Read these verses out of a children's Bible while the kids do their hands-on activity. After reading the verses, engage the kids by asking questions about the text. Below are some questions to get you started.

Lesson Time Verses
Matthew 21:1-3
Matthew 21:6-11

Discussion Questions
1. What did Jesus do for the people that made them want to celebrate?
2. What are some things Jesus has done for you?
3. Why do you think Jesus rode on a donkey instead of a horse?

DISCOVERING PRAYER

Snack time can be a great time to teach preschoolers about prayer. You can also take prayer requests, review previous prayer requests, and receive praise reports.

1. Jesus did a lot of amazing things when He was on the earth. The most amazing thing He did was rescue us from sin and give us the gift of salvation. Have any of you ever received the gift of salvation?
2. Do you know what it means to receive the gift of salvation?
3. Do any of you want to receive the gift of salvation?

LET'S CREATE!

Praise Rocks
Supplies Needed: Small rocks, paint, brushes, tape.
- Before class, prepare the rocks by making sure they are all clean.
- Take the tape and with small strips, tape words like "Praise", "Jesus", and "Holy" on the rocks. You can also do this with a marker after the kids are done and the paint is dry.
- At craft time, let each child pick a rock.
- Let them paint the rock how they like.
- When the paint is mostly dry, peel the tape off to reveal the word on the rock.

Fancy Shaker Eggs
Supplies Needed: Plastic Easter eggs, colorful electrical tape, rice and/or beans, stickers.
- Place bowls of beans/rice on the table.
- Give each child two plastic eggs.
- Let them fill the eggs and close them.
- Help the kids tape the eggs shut.
- Let the kids decorate their eggs with stickers.
- Turn some music on and let the kids use their new instruments.

LESSON 3: THE LAST SUPPER

Supplies Needed for this Lesson:

Tissues
Crackers or Bagel
Colored Paper
Costumes
Misc. Craft Supplies
Chairs
Juice
Glue
Music
Play Food
Tub of Water
Tissue Paper
Plastic Wine Glasses
Costumes
Towels
String

LET'S PLAY A GAME!

Individual Play

A Little Help Freeze "Tag"
Supplies Needed: Tissues.
- Give each child a tissue.
- Have the kids put the tissue on their head.
- Tell the kids they cannot touch their own tissue.
- Turn some music on.
- Have the kids walk around the room with the tissue on their head.
- If their tissue falls off, the child has to freeze until another child picks up the tissue and puts it back on their head.
- If there is only one child in class, or if everyone is frozen, then the teacher can be the helper.

Multiple Play

Cooperative Musical Chairs
Supplies Needed: Chairs, music.
- Place chairs in a line, back to back with one less chair than there are children.
- Turn the music on and have the kids walk around the chairs.
- When the music stops, the kids have to find a chair, but they must find a way for all the kids to have a seat.
- When they've accomplished this, take one chair away.
- Continue with the game until all the kids can no longer figure out how to all have a seat.
- Encourage the kids to use kind words and help each other.

MEMORY VERSE

Read the memory verse to the kids, showing them the hand motions to help them learn it. Have the kids repeat the verse with you a couple times while doing the hand motions.

Anyone – Wave your hand in front of you.
Who calls on the name – Put your hands up to your mouth as if shouting.
Of the Lord – Point up.
Will be saved – Cross your hands over each other as though they're handcuffed, then pull them apart.

> Copy and cut out the memory verse cards for this month so the kids can take them home to practice!

LET'S LEARN GOD'S WORD!

Teacher Preparation
Before class, choose one of the following Hands-On Activities for the kids to do while you read the story.

The Last Supper
Supplies Needed: Crackers or bagel, juice, tub of water, paper towels.

- Have the kids sit at the table. Explain that before Jesus died on the cross He had a special meal with His friends that we call the Last Supper.
- Read the story from Matthew 26:26-28.
- After you read about the bread, hand out the element. Tell the kids not to eat it yet.
- After you read about the wine, hand out the juice, but tell the kids not to drink it yet.
- Explain that Jesus wanted His followers to remember this special meal because it reminds us of what He did on the cross.
- Ask if any of the kids want to pray and thank God for what He did on the cross. After praying, tell the kids to eat the bread. When they're done, have all the kids drink the juice. After the communion, tell the kids that Jesus also washed the feet of His friends.
- Ask the kids if they know why Jesus would do that.
- Explain that Jesus wanted to show His friends they should be servants to other people. He showed them how to serve others by washing their feet.
- Explain that feet washing was important in Jesus' day. This is because everyone wore sandals and it was very dusty and dirty. Since they walked everywhere they had to wash their feet often.
- Put their feet in the tub of water and then dry them off.
- Ask the kids how it made them feel getting their feet washed. Explain that sometimes it's hard to let people serve you, but it's a good thing too. Ask the kids to come up with ways they can serve others.

LET'S LEARN GOD'S WORD!

Acting the Part
Supplies Needed: Costumes (optional), play food.
Have the kids act out the scenes as you read an expanded version of the last supper.

Read these verses out of a children's Bible while the kids do their hands-on activity. After reading the verses, engage the kids by asking questions about the text. Below are some questions to get you started.

Lesson Time Verses
John 13:4-5
John 13: 12-15
John 13:21, 26
Matthew 26:26-29

Discussion Questions

1. How do you think Jesus felt knowing one of his friends was going to do something really mean to him?
2. Do you remember what the bread meant?
3. Do you remember what the wine meant?
4. Why did Jesus tell his followers to "Do this to remember Me"?
5. Do you think Jesus was happy or sad in this story? Why?

DISCOVERING PRAYER!

Snack time can be a great time to teach preschoolers about prayer. You can also take prayer requests, review previous prayer requests, and receive praise reports.

1. Does God like it when we pray?
2. Why do you think it's important to pray?
3. I bet Jesus prayed for Judas even though He knew Judas was going to do something mean to him. Do you think we should pray for people who have done mean things to us?

LET'S CREATE!

Last Supper Picture
Supplies Needed: Blank pieces of colored paper, copies of plate and glass picture from page 62, colored tissue paper, and glue.
- Give each child a blank paper, and a copy of the plate and glass. Help the kids cut the plate and glass out.
- Have the kids rip small pieces of colored tissue paper up and glue pieces of 'bread' on the plate and fill the glass with 'wine'.

Wine Glass Craft
Supplies Needed: Plastic wine glasses, string, miscellaneous craft decorations, and glue.
- Give each child a plastic wine glass.
- Let the kids decorate their glasses by gluing string around it and other decorations such as stick on jewels.

LAST SUPPER PICTURE

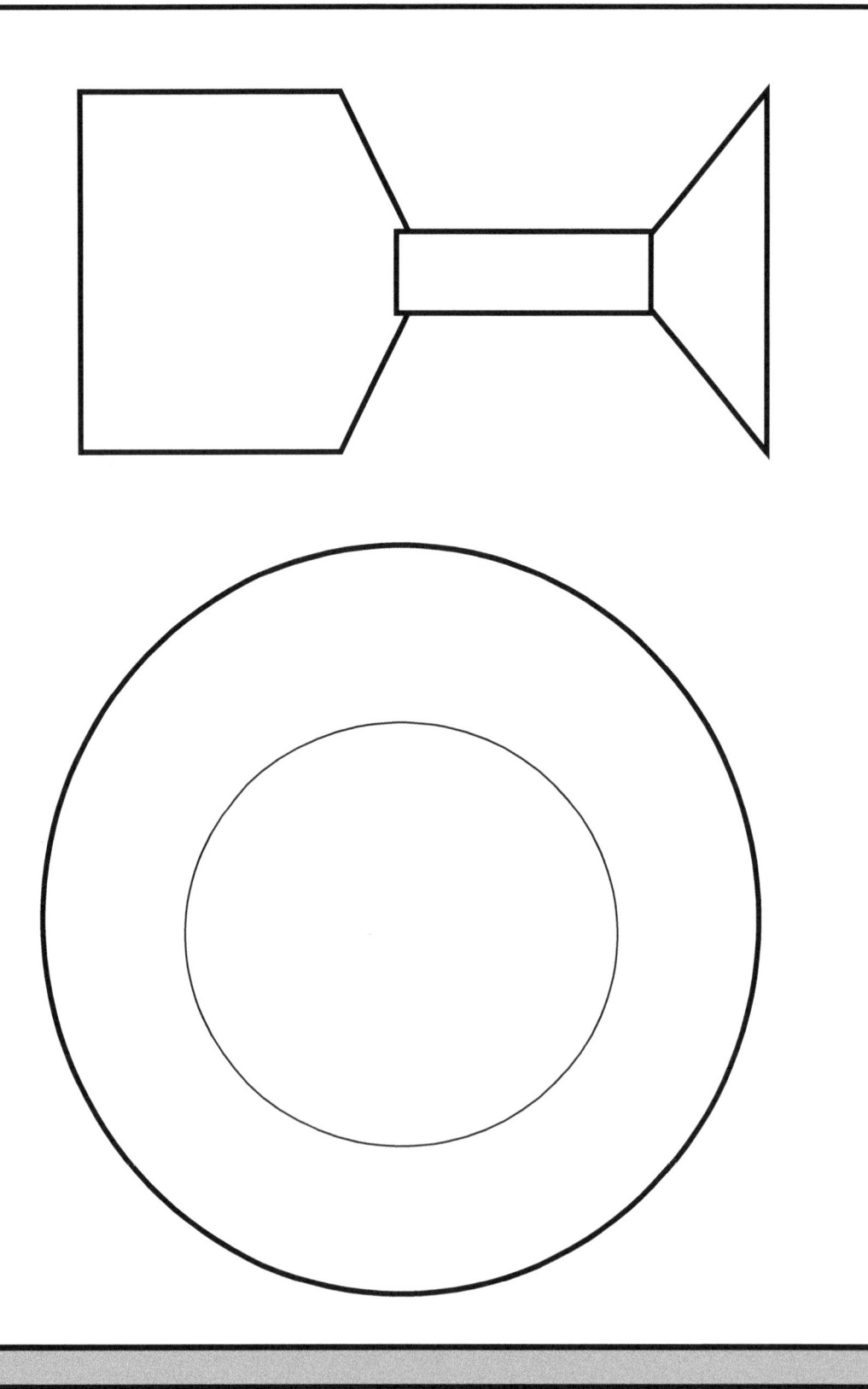

LESSON 4: JESUS' DEATH & RESURRECTION

Supplies Needed for this Lesson:

Masking Tape	Plastic Eggs	Strips of Cloth	Paint
Resurrection Egg Set	Costumes	Painter's Tape	Glue
Paint Brushes	Paint Smocks	Egg Cartons	Paper

LET'S PLAY A GAME!

Individual Play

In the Tomb, Out of the Tomb
Supplies Needed: Masking tape.
- Make a line on the ground with the masking tape.
- Tell the kids that one side is 'in the tomb' and the other side is 'out of the tomb'.
- Line the kids up on the tape. Begin yelling out "in the tomb" or "out of the tomb".
- The kids must jump to the correct side. Kids can be out if they jump to the wrong side.
- Make sure the kids are all jumping to the correct side when it's called out. Play as long as you wish, or for allotted time.

Multiple Play

Hot Egg
Supplies Needed: Plastic Easter eggs, pieces of cloth.
- Before class, fill several plastic eggs with small pieces of cloth. Leave one egg empty.
- Have all the kids sit in a circle and give every other child one of the eggs.
- Tell the kids not to open the eggs until told to.
- Start playing some music and have the kids pass the eggs around the circle until the music stops.
- When the music stops, the kids holding the eggs can open them.
- The child who has the empty egg will shout "The Tomb is Empty!".
- The other children will then shout "He is risen!".

MEMORY VERSE

Read the memory verse to the kids, showing them the hand motions to help them learn it. Have the kids repeat the verse with you a couple times while doing the hand motions.

Anyone – Wave your hand in front of you.
Who calls on the name – Put your hands up to your mouth as if shouting.
Of the Lord – Point up.
Will be saved – Cross your hands over each other as though they're handcuffed, then pull them apart.

> Copy and cut out the memory verse cards for this month so the kids can take them home to practice!

LET'S LEARN GOD'S WORD!

Teacher Preparation
Before class, choose one of the following Hands-On Activities for the kids to do while you read the story.

Resurrection Egg Hunt
Supplies Needed: Resurrection egg set.
- Before class, hide the eggs around the room.
- Have the kids search for the eggs.
- When all the eggs have been found have the kids sit in a circle.
- Go through the paper that comes with the set and tell what all the items in the eggs represent.

Acting the Part
Supplies Needed: Costumes (optional).
- Let the kids act out the story as you read it.

Read these verses out of a children's Bible while the kids do their hands-on activity. After reading the verses, engage the kids by asking questions about the text. Below are some questions to get you started.

Lesson Time Verses
Matthew 27:27-29
Matthew 27:35-37
Matthew 27:45, 50
Matthew 27:59-61
Matthew 28:1-10

Discussion Questions

1. Are you happy Jesus came back to life and we can talk with Him whenever we want?
2. Did you know Jesus didn't have to go through any of that?
3. He could have prayed for angels to come and rescue him from the hands of those mean people, but He didn't! Why do you think that is?
4. He loves us so much He was willing to go through all those mean things those people did to Him. Isn't that amazing? He did all that because He loves you and me!
5. We've been talking about the gift of salvation. Did you know it's because of what Jesus went through in our story today, that we are able to receive that gift?

DISCOVERING PRAYER

Snack time can be a great time to teach preschoolers about prayer. You can also take prayer requests, review previous prayer requests, and receive praise reports.

1. Would anyone like to pray and thank Jesus for all the things He went through so we could have the gift of salvation?
2. Have any of you received the gift of salvation before?
3. Would any of you like to receive that gift today?

LET'S CREATE!

Cross Painting
Supplies Needed: Paper, paint, painter's tape, brushes, paint smocks.
- Before class, prepare several pieces of blank paper by taking painter's tape and taping a cross on the paper.
- Give each child a paper with the taped cross on it.
- Let the kids paint their paper the way they want without taking the tape off.
- When the paint has dried, take the tape off and show the kids their cross.

Egg Carton Cross
Supplies Needed: Egg cartons, paint, brushes, paint smocks, glue.
- Before class, cut egg cartons in half lengthwise. Cut some of the halves in half so that there are some with six bumps and some with three.
- Give each child one six piece and one three piece.
- Let the kids paint their cartons.
- Show the kids how to make a cross with their cartons by putting the three piece on top of the six piece.
- Glue the pieces together.

LESSON 5: WHAT JESUS DID WHILE IN THE GRAVE

Supplies Needed for this Lesson:

Resurrection Egg Set	Crumpled Paper	Popsicle Sticks	Paint
Super Hero Masks	Shields	Cardstock	Glue
Butcher Paper	Paint Brushes	Paint Smocks	Green Paper

LET'S PLAY A GAME!

Individual Play

Resurrection Egg Hunt
Supplies Needed: Resurrection egg set.
- Hide the Resurrection eggs around the room, before class.
- Let the kids search for the eggs, open them and see if they know what all the pieces mean.

Multiple Play

Victory in Jesus
Supplies Needed: Crumpled up pieces of paper, shields.
- Give each child a shield.
- Tell the kids that the balls of paper are 'sin' and 'death'.
- Explain that when Jesus was in the grave, He defeated sin and death and gave us the power to defeat sin and death too.
- Throw the balls of paper at the kids and let them dodge and fight them off.

MEMORY VERSE

Read the memory verse to the kids, showing them the hand motions to help them learn it. Have the kids repeat the verse with you a couple times while doing the hand motions.

Anyone – Wave your hand in front of you.
Who calls on the name – Put your hands up to your mouth as if shouting.
Of the Lord – Point up.
Will be saved – Cross your hands over each other as though they're handcuffed, then pull them apart.

> Copy and cut out the memory verse cards for this month so the kids can take them home to practice!

LET'S LEARN GOD'S WORD!

Teacher Preparation
Before class, choose one of the following Hands-On Activities for the kids to do while you read the story.

Super Hero Party
Supplies Needed: Super Hero masks, signs of 'death' and 'sin' on cardstock.
- Before class, set up signs around the room that have 'death' and 'sin' and other bad things on them.
- Give each child a Super Hero mask.
- Tell the children that God has made them all Super Hero's. They can defend themselves against sin, death, sickness and other bad things.
- Let the kids 'beat up' the signs as their Super Hero selves.

Discussion Questions

1. What have we learned this month about Jesus?
2. Do you remember what the first sin was?
3. Who committed the first sin?
4. What happened on Palm Sunday?
5. Why were the people so happy that Jesus had come into town on Palm Sunday?
6. What kind of mean things did people do to Jesus?
7. Did Jesus have to go through all that?
8. Why did he choose to go through all those mean things?
9. What gift does Jesus offer us since He took care of sin?

DISCOVERING PRAYER

Snack time can be a great time to teach preschoolers about prayer. You can also take prayer requests, review previous prayer requests, and receive praise reports from the kids.

1. Do you think it's important to pray and ask God to help us not do wrong things?
2. Do you think it's important to pray to God after we've done something wrong?

LET'S CREATE!

Paint a Picture
Supplies Needed: Paint, paint smocks, brushes, butcher paper.
- Give each child a small piece of butcher paper.
- Help the kids tape their paper to the wall.
- Tell the kids to paint a picture of something from the Easter story.

Palm Branch
Supplies Needed: Popsicle sticks, small strips of green paper, glue.
- Scatter small strips of paper on the table.
- Give each child one or two Popsicle sticks.
- Let the kids glue 'leaves' on their 'branches'.
- Kids can make more than one if they want.

MARCH MEMORY VERSE CARDS

Romans 10:13

"Anyone who calls on the name of the Lord will be saved."

Romans 10:13

"Anyone who calls on the name of the Lord will be saved."

Romans 10:13

"Anyone who calls on the name of the Lord will be saved."

Romans 10:13

"Anyone who calls on the name of the Lord will be saved."

Romans 10:13

"Anyone who calls on the name of the Lord will be saved."

Romans 10:13

"Anyone who calls on the name of the Lord will be saved."

Romans 10:13

"Anyone who calls on the name of the Lord will be saved."

Romans 10:13

"Anyone who calls on the name of the Lord will be saved."

APRIL
GOD'S MIGHTY WARRIORS!

OVERVIEW

Society teaches us that a mighty warrior is big, strong and sometimes has a superpower. But the Bible teaches us that God's warriors come in all shapes and sizes and usually don't have many special talents at all. In these lessons, we will look at some of God's Mighty Warriors.

Memory Verse

Isaiah 43:5
"Do not be afraid because I am with you."

Hand Motions

Do Not
Hold up one finger and wiggle it back and forth.

Be Afraid
Cross arms, hunch over and look scared.

Because I am
Point up.

With you
Point to someone.

LESSON 1: David & Goliath
The story of David and Goliath is a classic story taught to kids. This lesson will explore the idea that even though the children are small, they can still do big things for God.

LESSON 2: Samson
God gave Samson his strength and even though Samson took that strength for granted, God still used him in mighty ways. This lesson will explore what God's strength looks like in our lives today.

LESSON 3: God's Armor for Us
Based on Ephesians 6:10-18 this lesson will teach what the armor of God looks like in our lives and what the purpose of each piece is for.

LESSON 4: Gideon the Scared Soldier
Gideon can be such a fun story to tell children. This lesson will explore why Gideon was afraid and relate it to fears the kids might have. Even though we have fears, God is able to help us work through those fears and make us mighty warriors.

LESSON 5: Joshua and the Big Wall
Joshua was raised to be a warrior for God, to fight those that stood in the way of God's promises. But in this battle, God had Joshua march in silence. This lesson will explore the idea that sometimes God wants us to be warriors in ways we don't understand.

LESSON 1: DAVID & GOLIATH

Supplies Needed for this Lesson:

Bowls	Two Large Rocks	Cotton Balls	String
Ball of Used Tape	Towels	Ten Small Rocks	Ice
Type of Target	Crumpled Paper	Bean Bags	Costumes
Electric Tape	Y Shaped Sticks	Acrylic Paint	Glue
Paint Brushes	Paint Smocks	Popsicle Sticks	Crayons
Enough Small Stones for Each Child to have Five		Large Rubber Bands	

LET'S PLAY A GAME!

Individual Play

Bravery Bowls

Supplies Needed: Bowls, ice, cotton balls, string, ball of 'used' tape, or other objects and towels.

- Before class, put the items into different bowls and cover them with towels.
- When the game starts, tell the kids they will need to try and figure out what is in each bowl without looking. Tell the kids it could be slimy or sticky and ask them if they're brave enough for the task.
- Tell the kids they are not allowed to make any guesses until everyone has touched the item.
- Let each child slide their hand under one of the towels.
- Once each child has had a chance to feel the object, have them guess what it is. Once they've all guessed, uncover the bowl and show them the object.
- Continue will all the bowls.

Multiple Play

David & Goliath

Supplies Needed: Ten small flat rocks and two larger flat rocks, painted if desired.

- Split the kids into two teams. Show the kids the larger rocks. These are Goliath.
- Place the Goliath rocks at the end of a table. If you have two tables to use that would be best. This can also work on uncarpeted floors.
- Give each team five rocks. If there are more than five kids on each team, you will need to collect the rocks again.
- Each child will get one shot to try and knock the Goliath rock off the table by sliding, not throwing, their rock across the table.
- Game ends when the rock is off the table or allotted time is up.
- See which team can knock Goliath off the table the most times.

MEMORY VERSE

Read the memory verse to the kids, showing them the hand motions to help them learn it. Have the kids repeat the verse with you a couple times while doing the hand motions.

Do not – Hold up one finger and wiggle it back and forth.
Be afraid – Cross arms, hunch over and look scared.
Because I am – Point up.
With you – Point to someone.

> Copy and cut out the memory verse cards for this month so the kids can take them home to practice!

LET'S LEARN GOD'S WORD!

Teacher Preparation
Before class, choose one of the following Hands-On Activities for the kids to do while you read the story.

Acting the Part
Supplies Needed: Costumes (optional), Goliath target, bean bags.
- Have the kids act out the story as you read it.
- Target can be a piece of cardboard with a bull's eye drawn on it.

Five Little Stones
Supplies Needed: Several smooth stones, acrylic paint, paint brushes, paint smocks.
- Give each child five small stones. Let the kids paint their rocks as you tell the story.

Read these verses out of a children's Bible while the kids do their hands-on activity. After reading the verses, engage the kids by asking questions about the text. Below are some questions to get you started.

Lesson Time Verses
1 Samuel 17:1, 4, 8-10	1 Samuel 17:26-27, 31-37
1 Samuel 17:17, 20	1 Samuel 17:40, 42-51
1 Samuel 17:22-25	

Discussion Questions

1. Why do you think the adults were afraid of Goliath, but David wasn't?
2. Do you ever feel like you're too young or too small to do things?
3. What kind of things would you do if you were bigger?
4. What are some things God can help us do?
5. Is praying for people something you could do for God right now?
6. What else can you do for God as young kids?

DISCOVERING PRAYER

Snack time can be a great time to teach preschoolers about prayer. You can also take prayer requests, review previous prayer requests, and receive praise reports from the kids.

1. In our lesson today, we talked about things we can do for God right now. Does anyone want to pray and ask God to help them be able to do those things without fear?
2. David was a mighty warrior for God. Did you know it's possible to be a mighty prayer warrior for God?
3. Why is it important to pray?

LET'S CREATE!

David's Sling
Supplies needed: Rubber bands, Y-shaped sticks, electrical tape, scrap paper crumpled up.
- Give each child a Y-shaped stick and a rubber band.
- Show the kids how to wrap the rubber bands around each 'Y' of the stick.
- Help them secure the rubber band to the stick with electrical tape.
- Let the kids use the crumpled up paper and take shots at a target or a picture of Goliath.

David & Goliath Stick Figures
Supplies Needed: Popsicle sticks, glue, crayons.
- After explaining how tall Goliath was, have the kids glue Popsicle sticks together to make a figure of themselves.
- Then, have them make a stick figure of how tall they think Goliath was compared to them.
- Sticks cut in half can be used for arms and legs, or scraps of paper can be used to make head and limbs.

LESSON 2: SAMSON

Supplies Needed for this Lesson:

Balloons   Stuffed Animals   Children's Bibles   Construction Cones
Costumes   Construction Paper   Scissors   Tape or Stapler
Potting Soil   Cat Grass   Googly Eyes   Clear Plastic Cups
Marker   Glue

LET'S PLAY A GAME!

Individual Play
Strength Training
Supplies Needed: Balloons.
- Before class, blow up enough balloons so each child will be able to have one.
- Let each child choose a balloon. They must try to pop their balloons, but they may only use their bodies, no objects can be used to help them.
- When the game is over ask the kids if it was hard to pop their balloons.

Multiple Play
Boot Camp
Supplies Needed: Stuffed animals, children's Bibles, construction cones.
- Before class, set up the construction cones in two straight lines, with a foot or so of space between each cone. Place a pile of stuffed animals somewhere in the room and stacks of children's Bibles, two tall, somewhere else in the room.
- When the game starts, tell the kids they are going to prove how strong they are.
- Have the kid's line up in two lines.
- The kids must weave back and forth through the cones without knocking any over.
- Go to the pile of stuffed animals and throw one as far as they can.
- Go to the pile of books, pick two up and carry them to the other side of the room.
- Then do three jumping jacks.
- Send two kids at a time and have the other children cheer them on.

MEMORY VERSE

Read the memory verse to the kids, showing them the hand motions to help them learn it. Have the kids repeat the verse with you a couple times while doing the hand motions.

Do not – Hold up one finger and wiggle it back and forth.
Be afraid – Cross arms, hunch over and look scared.
Because I am – Point up.
With you – Point to someone.

> Copy and cut out the memory verse cards for this month so the kids can take them home to practice!

LET'S LEARN GOD'S WORD!

Teacher Preparation
Before class, choose one of the following Hands-On Activities for the kids to do while you read the story.

Acting the Part
Supplies Needed: Costumes (optional).
- Have the kids act out the scenes in the story as you read it to them.

Talent Show
Supplies Needed: Costumes (optional).
- Tell the kids they're going to learn about a man named Samson. God made him very strong.
- Ask the kids to think about what talents God has given them while the story is read.
- Tell the kids that after the story, they are going to put on a talent show to show what talents God has given them.
- This option can be used with the one above.

Read these verses out of a children's Bible while the kids do their hands-on activity. After reading the verses, engage the kids by asking questions about the text. Below are some questions to get you started.

Lesson Time Verses
Judges 16:4-9
Judges 16:10-12
Judges 16:13-14
Judges 16:15-19
Judges 16:21-30

Discussion Questions

1. Samson did a lot of things that he shouldn't have, but God still used him. Do you think God can use us even though we mess up sometimes?
2. What did Samson have to do to keep his strength?
3. What kinds of talents do you have?
4. Do you think God can use those talents? How?
5. Do you think Samson should have kept trusting Delilah? Why or Why not?
6. Did you know that we all carry God's power on the inside of us?
7. What kinds of things do you think we can do with that power?
8. If you were Samson, what would you have done differently?

DISCOVERING PRAYER!

Snack time can be a great time to teach preschoolers about prayer. You can also take prayer requests, review previous prayer requests, and receive praise reports.

1. Why does God give us talents?
2. What talents would you like God to use?
3. Who would like to pray and ask God to use their talents in a special way?

Let's Create!

Samson's Hair
Supplies Needed: Brown and black construction paper, scissors, tape, stapler or glue.
- Before class, cut out long strips of different colored construction paper.
- Measure each child's head with the construction paper and cut out a thick strip.
- Let the kids glue colored strips of paper to the sides of the brown strip, leaving the middle open.
- Staple, glue or tape the brown paper to form a circle and let the kids wear Samson's hair.

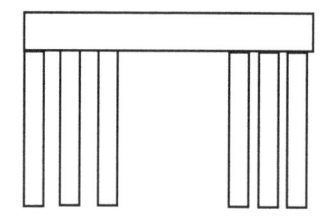

Sampson's Hair Garden
Supplies Needed: Clear plastic cups, potting soil, cat grass, googly eyes, marker, glue.
- Give each child a cup.
- Have them fill it with potting soil.
- Give each child some seeds to plant in their cup.
- Let the kids decorate their cups by gluing eyes and drawing face parts on it.
- Let the kids take their plants home, to watch Samson's hair grow.

LESSON 3: GOD'S ARMOR FOR US

Supplies Needed for this Lesson:

2 Pairs of Large Kids Boots
2 Large Kids Jackets
2 Pictures of a Bad Guy
Toy Shield or Cardboard Box
Plastic Helmet
Crayons
Glue
Paint Brushes

2 Large Kids Vests
2 Hats
Small Bag or Pillowcase
Plastic Breast Plate
Plastic Shield
Cardstock
Marker
Paint Smocks

2 Kids Belts
Stick
Balloons
Plastic Sword
Paper
Scissors
Paint
Tape

LET'S PLAY A GAME!

Individual Play

Punching Bag Practice

Supplies Needed: A small bag or pillowcase, balloons, toy shield or cardboard box.

- Before class, fill a small bag or pillowcase with blown up balloons.
- Tell the kids that without armor it's easy for us to get hurt.
- Let the kids hit or punch the bag full of balloons. Point out that it's soft and squishy and if it were a human, that human would be in a lot of pain right now.
- Put the shield or cardboard box in front of the bag of balloons. Let the kids try hitting the bag again. Point out that the shield is hard and protects the bag from being injured. Explain that God has given us armor to use so we don't get hurt.

Multiple Play

Armor Relay

Supplies Needed: 2 or more of each: large kids boots, vest, belt, jacket, hat, stick, picture of a bad guy.

- Break the kids into two groups, more if there are a lot of kids.
- Have the clothes piled on the floor a few feet away from the picture of the bad guy.
- Tell the kids, they will need to pull all the clothes on, run to the picture, hit it with the stick, run back and take all the clothes off.
- All the kids will need to do this.
- The team that gets through the challenge first, wins.

MEMORY VERSE

Read the memory verse to the kids, showing them the hand motions to help them learn it. Have the kids repeat the verse with you a couple times while doing the hand motions.

Do not – Hold up one finger and wiggle it back and forth.
Be afraid – Cross arms, hunch over and look scared.
Because I am – Point up.
With you – Point to someone.

> Copy and cut out the memory verse cards for this month so the kids can take them home to practice!

LET'S LEARN GOD'S WORD!

Teacher Preparation
Before class, choose one of the following Hands-On Activities for the kids to do while you read the story.

Armor Object Lesson
Supplies Needed: Belt, oversized kids boots, plastic shield, plastic breast plate, plastic sword, plastic helmet.
- Hand out the items to the kids so that each child has one piece of armor. If there are more kids than armor, hand it out to the older kids, or have more than one set of armor.
- Tell the kids with the armor, they are going to have a battle and their only protection is the piece of armor they have.
- Have the kids 'battle'. Remind them to only pretend to hit each other.

Draw a Soldier
Supplies Needed: Paper, crayons.
- Give each child a piece of paper.
- Have them draw and color a soldier.
- As you read the story, have the kids add the armor to their soldier and place it where they think it should go.

Read these verses out of a children's Bible while the kids do their hands-on activity. After reading the verses, engage the kids by asking questions about the text. On the next page are some questions to get you started.

Lesson Time Verses	
Ephesians 6:11-13	Ephesians 6:16
Ephesians 6:14	Ephesians 6:17
Ephesians 6:15	Ephesians 6:18

LET'S LEARN GOD'S WORD!

Discussion Questions

1. What do you think the belt of truth is for? Why is it important for us to tell the truth?
2. How does the breast plate help us?
3. Why do you think God wants us to protect our hearts?
4. Have you ever walked outside barefoot and stubbed your toe? It hurts right? Do you think that's why God wants us to wear shoes of peace?
5. What does it mean to have peace?
6. Do you think God wants us to have peace wherever we go?
7. What does the shield protect us from?
8. The shield helps protect us from flying objects, like arrows. Why do you think we need a shield of faith? What do you think faith is?
9. Sometimes we can have thoughts come to us that the devil put there. Like "I'm not good enough" or "God can't use me", but when we read our Bible, we find out those are lies. Do you think we can use our shield of faith to battle those thoughts?
10. What does the helmet protect? Why do you think God wants us to protect our heads?
11. Do your parents tell you there are certain movies or shows you can't watch? That's because they're making sure bad things don't get into your mind. If we keep the helmet of Salvation on, then we are protecting what goes into our minds.
12. What does the sword help us do?
13. What do you think the sword of the spirit is?
14. When we get saved, God sends the Holy Spirit to help us. We can ask him to help us fight when we need to. We can also arm ourselves with the sword of the Spirit by learning God's Word. Do you think you are all arming yourselves with the sword of the spirit right now?

DISCOVERING PRAYER!

Snack time can be a great time to teach preschoolers about prayer. You can also take prayer requests, review previous prayer requests, and receive praise reports.

1. Do you think it's ok to pray and ask God to help us remember to keep His armor on?
2. When the Bible is read to you, do you think you can pray and ask God to help you understand the story better?
3. Does anyone want to pray and ask God to help them understand the Bible better right now?

LET'S CREATE!

Shoes of Peace
Supplies Needed: Cardstock, marker, crayons, glue, and scissors.
- Trace the kids feet, with shoes on, onto card stock.
- Help the kids cut out the shapes.
- Cut out a strip of cardstock and help the kids glue it on as a strap by folding the ends under the shoe and gluing the flaps to the bottom. The strap will fit over their feet like sandals.
- Let the kids decorate their shoes with crayons.

Paint a Picture
Supplies Needed: Paper, paint, paint smocks, brushes, and tape.
- Give each child a small piece of butcher paper.
- Tape their paper to the wall.
- Have the kids paint a picture of themselves wearing the armor of God.

LESSON 4: GIDEON THE SCARED SOLDIER

Supplies Needed for this Lesson:

Costumes	White or Black Paper	Orange & Red Tissue Paper
Glue	Tape	No-Bake Clay
Paint	Paint Brushes	Paint Smocks

LET'S PLAY A GAME!

Individual Play
Gideon, Gideon Do This
Supplies Needed: None.
- Play this game like "Simon Says". The kids are Gideon and they must listen for God's voice.
- After saying "Gideon, Gideon do this", have the kids do various things, such as jumping, hopping on one foot, dancing, etc.
- Every now and then give a command without saying the phrase. If the kids follow it, they are out.

Multiple Play
Hide and Seek
Supplies Needed: None.
- Tell the kids they will be learning about one of God's warriors who was very afraid.
- Tell the kids they are going to play a game of hide and seek.
- Explain that Gideon hid from the people who were trying to hurt his people.

MEMORY VERSE

Read the memory verse to the kids, showing them the hand motions to help them learn it. Have the kids repeat the verse with you a couple times while doing the hand motions.

Do not – Hold up one finger and wiggle it back and forth.
Be afraid – Cross arms, hunch over and look scared.
Because I am – Point up.
With you – Point to someone.

> Copy and cut out the memory verse cards for this month so the kids can take them home to practice!

LET'S LEARN GOD'S WORD!

Teacher Preparation
Before class, choose one of the following Hands-On Activities for the kids to do while you read the story.

Scary Stories
Supplies Needed: None.
- Have the kids tell you things they're afraid of like, the dark, bugs, fire, etc.
- Tell the kids that even though they have things they're afraid of God can still use them in mighty ways.
- Talk about how God used Gideon, even though he was afraid.
- Talk about how God will help overcome our fears so we can do what God wants us to.

Acting the Part
Supplies Needed: Costumes (optional).
- Have the kids act out the scenes as you read the story.

Read these verses out of a children's Bible while the kids do their hands-on activity. After reading the verses, engage the kids by asking questions about the text. Below are some questions to get you started.

Lesson Time Verses
Judges 6:14-23   Judges 7:9-15
Judges 6:33-38   Judges 7:16-22

Discussion Questions
1. Why do you think Gideon was hiding from the Midianites?
2. Gideon told the angel he was the least important person in his family and he couldn't do the job. Are you the youngest, or one of the youngest people in your family?
3. Does it sometimes seem as though you can't do a lot of things because you're one of the youngest?
4. Gideon did several tests to make sure he was really hearing from God. How do we know if we're really hearing from God?
5. Gideon was afraid to help God at first because he didn't think he was the best choice. Later he was afraid because he wasn't sure God was really telling him to do something. But God made sure Gideon knew He would help Gideon. Do you think God will help us when we're afraid?
6. What can you do if you're afraid?

DISCOVERING PRAYER

Snack time can be a great time to teach preschoolers about prayer. You can also take prayer requests, review previous prayer requests, and receive praise reports.

1. Do you think there are things you need to be protected from?
2. What can we ask God to protect us from?
3. Do you think God can help you not be afraid anymore?
4. Are there any fears you would like to pray about today?

LET'S CREATE!

Gideon's Torch
Supplies Needed: White or black paper, tape, red, orange and yellow tissue paper, glue.
- Give each child a piece of white or black paper.
- Help the kids roll their paper into a tube and tape it. You can have one end be wider than the other, to give it a torch look.
- Give the kids scraps of tissue paper.
- Help them put a layer of glue on the inside of one end of their torch.
- Show the kids how to stuff the tissue paper inside to make it look like fire.

Candle Holders
Supplies Needed: No-bake clay, paint, paint brushes, paint smocks.
- Give each child a small ball of clay.
- Have them create a candle holder.
- Explain that Gideon and his army used torches and the candle holders will be like torches for our homes.
- Let the craft dry.
- If the project dries in time, let the kids paint their candle holders or encourage them to paint them at home with their parents.

LESSON 5: JOSHUA AND THE BIG WALL

Supplies Needed for this Lesson:

Building Blocks	Bean Bags	Toy People	Costumes
Several Small Boxes	String	Tape	Paper
Construction Paper	Glue	Crayons	Plastic Knives
Marshmallows	Frosting		

LET'S PLAY A GAME!

Individual Play
Follow the Leader
Supplies Needed: None.
- Explain that Joshua had instructions from God to walk around a city without talking.
- Have the kids play follow the leader.
- Play the game once as normal.
- Play the game a second time, but without using words.
- See if the kids will still follow what you do even if you don't say it.

Multiple Play
Knock Down the Walls
Supplies Needed: Small building blocks, bean bags.
- Divide the kids into two groups.
- Give each group some blocks to build with on a table.
- Tell them to build a tower as strong as they can.
- When the towers are built, give each team some bean bags.
- Have the kids slide bean bags across the table to knock the other team's tower down.
- The team who can keep their tower standing wins.

MEMORY VERSE

Read the memory verse to the kids, showing them the hand motions to help them learn it. Have the kids repeat the verse with you a couple times while doing the hand motions.

Do not – Hold up one finger and wiggle it back and forth.
Be afraid – Cross arms, hunch over and look scared.
Because I am – Point up.
With you – Point to someone.

> Copy and cut out the memory verse cards for this month so the kids can take them home to practice!

LET'S LEARN GOD'S WORD!

Teacher Preparation
Before class, choose one of the following Hands-On Activities for the kids to do while you read the story.

Acting the Part
Supplies Needed: Costumes (optional), several small boxes, string, and tape.
- Before class, tape three small boxes together so they sit in a row. Tape a piece of string to the bottom of the boxes. Have it be long enough where you can reach it and pull it.
- Have other boxes ready to go for the kids to build the rest of the wall.
- When it comes time for the wall to fall down, pull the string, before the kids can knock it over.

Create a Story
Supplies Needed: Small toy people, building blocks.
- Have all the items on the table.
- Have the kids work together to build a wall.
- Give each child a toy person.
- Tell the kids they are the army of Israel.
- As you read the story, let the kids act the story out with the toys.

Read these verses out of a children's Bible while the kids do their hands-on activity. After reading the verses, engage the kids by asking questions about the text. Below are some questions to get you started.

Lesson Time Verses
Joshua 5:13-15	Joshua 6:14
Joshua 6:1-5	Joshua 6:15
Joshua 6:8-10	Joshua 6:16-20
Joshua 6:11	

Discussion Questions

1. Why do you think God wanted Joshua and his army to march around the city of Jericho so many times in silence?
2. What do you think the people in the city were thinking when Joshua and his army were marching around the city in silence?
3. Do you think it was hard for them to march in silence?
4. How long do you think it took for them to march around a whole city?
5. Do you think you could march that long if God asked you to? Would you try?
6. Do you think it surprised all the people in the city when the army shouted on the last day of marching?

DISCOVERING PRAYER

Snack time can be a great time to teach preschoolers about prayer. You can also take prayer requests, review previous prayer requests, and receive praise reports.

1. What are some things we can talk about with God when we pray?
2. When can we pray?
3. Who can we pray for?
4. Do your parents ever take you to boring places where you have to wait a long time?
5. Do you think those are good times to pray?

LET'S CREATE!

Crumbled Wall Art
Supplies Needed: Paper, construction paper cut into squares, crayons, glue.
- Give each child a piece of paper.
- Scatter the squares in the middle of the table.
- Have the kids glue squares on their paper to represent a crumbled wall.
- Have the kids draw pictures of people next to the wall.

Marshmallow Walls
Supplies Needed: Marshmallows, plastic knives, frosting.
- Place bowls of marshmallows and a couple tubs of frosting on the table.
- Have the kids 'glue' their marshmallows together with the frosting to build a wall.

APRIL MEMORY VERSE CARDS

Isaiah 43:5
"Do not be afraid because I am with you."

Isaiah 43:5
"Do not be afraid because I am with you."

Isaiah 43:5
"Do not be afraid because I am with you."

Isaiah 43:5
"Do not be afraid because I am with you."

Isaiah 43:5
"Do not be afraid because I am with you."

Isaiah 43:5
"Do not be afraid because I am with you."

Isaiah 43:5
"Do not be afraid because I am with you."

Isaiah 43:5
"Do not be afraid because I am with you."

MAY
WHAT IS PRAYER?

OVERVIEW

Prayer is a vital part of having a relationship with God. These lessons will give the children a bigger view of prayer than the short weekly lessons provide.

Memory Verse

1 Thessalonians 5:17
"Never stop praying."

Hand Motions

Never
Hold up one finger and wiggle it back and forth.

Stop
Hold one hand out in front of you.

Praying
Fold hands in prayer.

LESSON 1: The Lord's Prayer
The Lord's Prayer is an outline for us to use when we pray. This lesson will explore the different parts of this outline. The kids will discover they really can pray about anything, anywhere, at any time.

LESSON 2: Daniel & The Lions
Daniel was a praying man and it got him into trouble. But God was on his side and because Daniel had a relationship with God, he knew God would protect him. This lesson will explore praying when you're in a tough situation.

LESSON 3: Hannah's Prayer
Hannah wanted a son so bad she continually went to the Lord to ask Him for a child. This lesson will explore praying for our hearts desires and who puts those desires in our hearts.

LESSON 4: Paul in Prison
Prison in Paul's day was no picnic, and he was there for doing God's work! This lesson will explore praying when life doesn't seem fair and praising God in the midst of trouble.

LESSON 5: Elijah's Prayer and a Contest
Elijah wanted to bring the people of Israel back to God because they were worshiping false gods. When it was his turn, he didn't dance around or cut himself. He simply prayed and God showed up. This lesson will explore the idea that prayer doesn't have to be showy to be effective.

LESSON 1: THE LORD'S PRAYER

Supplies Needed for this Lesson:

Ball	Big Bouncy Ball	Marker	Moldy Bread
Fresh Bread	Glue	Brads	Scissors
Crayons	Stickers	Paper	
Pictures that Connect with the Lord's Prayer		Throw & Tell Ball	

LET'S PLAY A GAME!

Individual Play

Get to Know You
Supplies Needed: Big bouncy ball and marker OR Throw and Tell ball.
- You can find "Throw & Tell" balls to buy or you can create your own with a bouncy ball and a marker. For Preschoolers a Throw and Tell ball has "get to know you" questions and pictures on it. For more information see page 234.
- Have the kids sit in a circle.
- Tell the kids you are going to throw the ball to someone.
- When they catch it, they have to pick something on the ball to tell about themselves.
- After they've told their story, all the kids say "Praise God for (child's name)".

Multiple Play

Thank You Game
Supplies Needed: Ball.
- Have the kids sit in a circle.
- Tell the kids, there are lots of things to be thankful for.
- Tell the kids that you are going to roll the ball to someone. Give them a category. Have them say something God made in that category.
- The child who receives the ball and answers will then roll the ball to someone else.
- Use the following categories: Food, people, nature, colors, and animals.

MEMORY VERSE

Read the memory verse to the kids, showing them the hand motions to help them learn it. Have the kids repeat the verse with you a couple times while doing the hand motions.

Never – Hold one finger up and wiggle it back and forth.
Stop – Hold one hand out in front you.
Praying – Fold hands together in prayer.

> Copy and cut out the memory verse cards for this month so the kids can take them home to practice!

LET'S LEARN GOD'S WORD!

Teacher Preparation
Before class, choose one of the following Hands-On Activities for the kids to do while you read the story.

Picture This
Supplies Needed: Pictures of things that connect with the Lord's Prayer. Things we can thank God for, things we can ask God for, things God can provide for us, things we can ask forgiveness for, etc.
- As you read through the Lord's Prayer, show the pictures to the kids.
- Have the kids try to match the pictures with the parts of the prayer.

Which Bread
Supplies Needed: Piece of moldy bread, piece of fresh bread.
- When talking about "our daily bread" you can use this object lesson.
- Show the kids the two pieces of bread.
- Explain that bread only stays fresh for a short period of time.
- Explain that we need to keep reading our Bibles so God's Word stays fresh in our minds. If we don't read the Word, it can get old and we can forget what we've learned. Just like bread gets moldy if we don't eat it.

Read these verses out of a children's Bible while the kids do their hands-on activity. After reading the verses, engage the kids by asking questions about the text. Below are some questions to get you started.

Lesson Time Verses
Matthew 6:9-13

Discussion Questions
1. What do you think it means to honor someone's name or keep it holy?
2. The Lord's Prayer tells us we should be thankful to God. What are some things we can thank Him for right now?
3. Let's put this part of the Lord's Prayer into practice. Who would like to pray first?
4. How do we know when God is talking to us?
5. What kinds of things do you think God wants to see happen on earth?
6. The Lord's Prayer tells us we should pray for things to happen on earth as they are in heaven. Who would like to put this part of the prayer into practice and pray for our family and friends who don't know God?
7. What are some things we need right now?
8. Who would like to put this part of the prayer into practice and pray for the needs of our classmates?

LET'S LEARN GOD'S WORD!

Discussion Questions Continued...

9. What is sin?
10. Why do we need forgiveness from sins?
11. Does anyone want to ask God for forgiveness for sins? If you don't want to say your sin out loud you can say a silent prayer to God for forgiveness.
12. Does anyone need to forgive a friend or family member for something they did?
13. Would anyone like to pray and tell God that you forgive that person?
14. What does it mean to be tempted?
15. What are some things you've been tempted to do?
16. Who wants to pray and ask God to help us from giving into temptation?

DISCOVERING PRAYER

Snack time can be a great time to teach preschoolers about prayer. You can also take prayer requests, review previous prayer requests, and receive praise reports.

1. What is the hardest part about praying?
2. When there is something we don't understand, do you think we can ask God to help us understand it?
3. What did you learn about prayer today that you didn't know before?

LET'S CREATE!

Prayer Wheel
Supplies Needed: Copies of the prayer wheel from page 92 and 93, glue, brads, crayons, stickers.
- Before class, cut out several of the templates and have them ready to go.
- Give each child a set of wheel templates.
- Place the partial wheel on top.
- Poke a brad through the middle.
- Let the kids decorate their wheels.

Lord's Prayer Handprint
Supplies Needed: Paper, marker, scissors, crayons, Lord's Prayer cut-out from page 94, glue.
- Have each child place their hands palms down on a piece of paper, making sure their fingers are all together. Have their hands side by side so their thumbs are touching. Trace around both hands, not between them.
- Help the kids cut out their hand print and fold it down the center to make a book.
- Help the kids glue the Lord's Prayer on the inside.
- Let the kids decorate their hands.

PRAYER WHEEL BOTTOM

- Give us what we need for today.
- Forgive our sins.
- Keep us from giving into temptation.
- Pray for my parents
- Pray for my Friends
- Pray for my neighbors.
- Thank God for what He's given
- Let Your will be done.

PRAYER WHEEL TOP

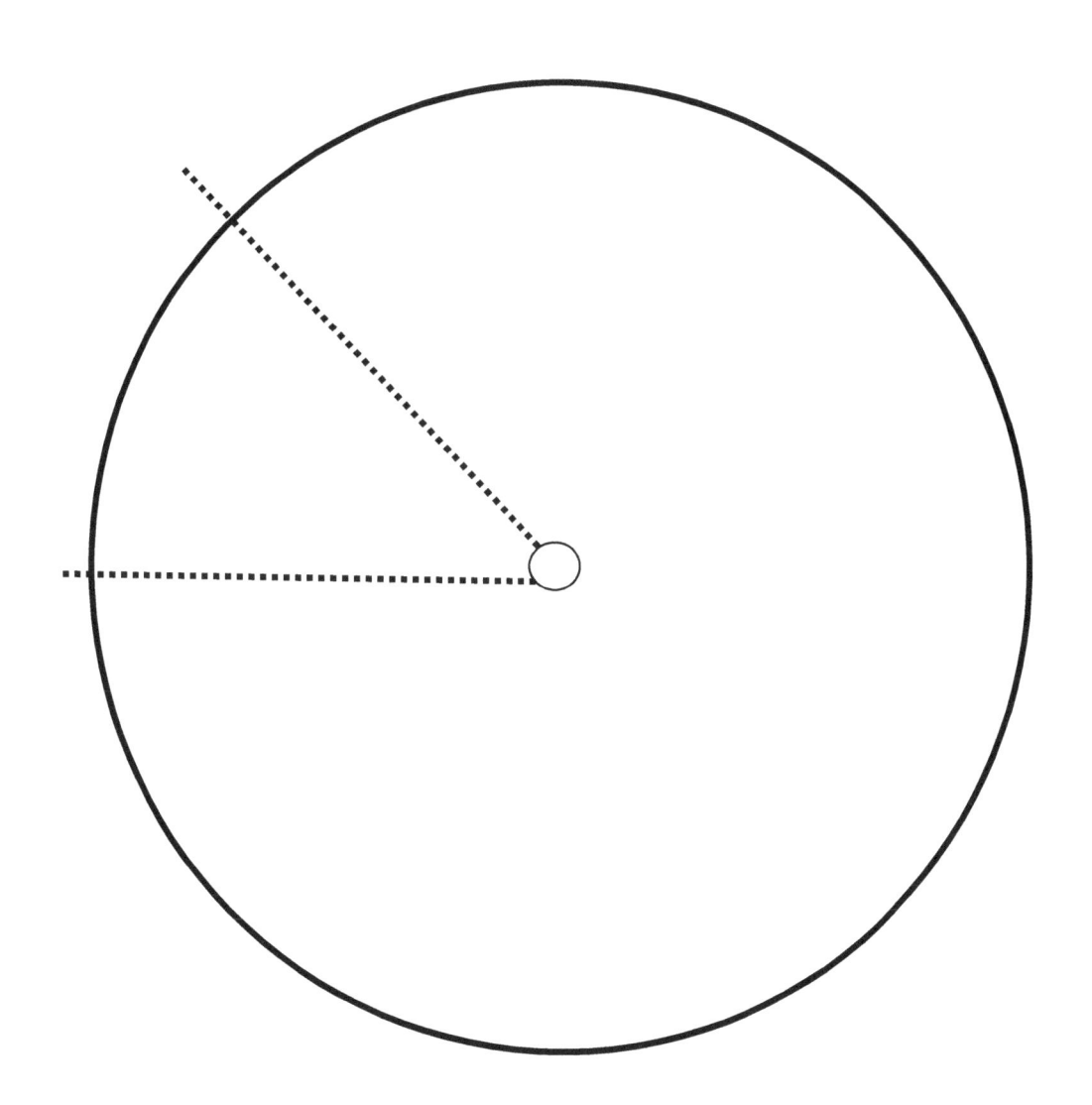

LORD'S PRAYER CUTOUTS

So this is how you should pray: 'Our Father in heaven we pray that your name will always be kept holy. We pray that your kingdom will come, that what you want will be done here on earth, the same as in heaven. Give us the food we need for today. Forgive our sins, just as we have forgiven those who did wrong to us. Don't let us be tempted, but save us from the Evil One.

So this is how you should pray: 'Our Father in heaven we pray that your name will always be kept holy. We pray that your kingdom will come, that what you want will be done here on earth, the same as in heaven. Give us the food we need for today. Forgive our sins, just as we have forgiven those who did wrong to us. Don't let us be tempted, but save us from the Evil One.

So this is how you should pray: 'Our Father in heaven we pray that your name will always be kept holy. We pray that your kingdom will come, that what you want will be done here on earth, the same as in heaven. Give us the food we need for today. Forgive our sins, just as we have forgiven those who did wrong to us. Don't let us be tempted, but save us from the Evil One.

So this is how you should pray: 'Our Father in heaven we pray that your name will always be kept holy. We pray that your kingdom will come, that what you want will be done here on earth, the same as in heaven. Give us the food we need for today. Forgive our sins, just as we have forgiven those who did wrong to us. Don't let us be tempted, but save us from the Evil One.

LESSON 2: DANIEL & THE LIONS

Supplies Needed for this Lesson:

Glass or Plastic Bottle
Paper Plates
Crayons
Plastic Knives
Misc. Craft Supplies
Small Figurine
Construction Paper
Undecorated Cookies
Cake Decorations
Paper
Glue
Frosting
Stickers
Costumes
Marker
Scissors

LET'S PLAY A GAME!

Individual Play

Daniel and the Lions
Supplies Needed: None.
- In this game the teacher is the angel who shuts the mouth of the lions.
- Have the kids pretend to be lions.
- Let them walk around, then yell "stop", like the angel stopped the mouths of the lions.
- The kids will have to freeze.
- If they move or make a sound, they have to sit down.
- Continue until all the kids are sitting down.

Multiple Play

Daniel, Daniel, Lion
Supplies Needed: None.
- Play this game like "Duck, Duck, Goose".
- Have the kids sit in a circle.
- Choose one person to be it.
- Have the child walk around the circle, touching each child's head.
- The child can choose to say either "Daniel" or "Lion" as they touch each child's head.
- When they say "Lion" the child who got tapped, will get up and chase the child around the circle. If the child who tapped them sits down in their spot before they are tagged, the child who got tagged will have to go around the circle.

MEMORY VERSE

Read the memory verse to the kids, showing them the hand motions to help them learn it. Have the kids repeat the verse with you a couple times while doing the hand motions.

Never – Hold one finger up and wiggle it back and forth.
Stop – Hold one hand out in front you.
Praying – Fold hands together in prayer.

> Copy and cut out the memory verse cards for this month so the kids can take them home to practice!

LET'S LEARN GOD'S WORD!

> ### Teacher Preparation
> Before class, choose one of the following Hands-On Activities for the kids to do while you read the story.

Acting the Part
Supplies Needed: Costumes (optional).
- Have the kids act out the scenes as you read them.

God's Protection
Supplies Needed: Glass bottle, small figure of a man, paper.
- Put the small figure of a man inside the bottle to represent Daniel.
- Crumple up a small piece of paper that fits just inside the neck of the bottle.
- Explain that the piece of paper is the lion trying to get at Daniel.
- Encourage the kids to blow in the bottle to get the lion near Daniel.
- The kids will find that instead of the paper going inside, it will actually come out of the bottle. This is because of the pressure that builds up behind it from their blowing.
- Explain to the kids that sometimes we come across people who only want to do us harm. God protects us in such a way that, no matter how hard people try to harm us, they won't be able to do much damage.

Read these verses out of a children's Bible while the kids do their hands-on activity. After reading the verses, engage the kids by asking questions about the text. Below are some questions to get you started.

Lesson Time Verses
Daniel 6:3-5	Daniel 6:15-18
Daniel 6:6-10	Daniel 6:19-23
Daniel 6:11-14	Daniel 6:24-26

Discussion Questions

1. How did prayer protect Daniel?
2. Why do you think the King wanted people to pray to him instead of God?
3. Daniel never did anything wrong which is why the other people had a hard time getting Daniel in trouble. Do you think it would be hard to never do anything wrong?
4. Do you think Daniel's ability to never do anything wrong had something to do with how much he prayed?
5. What do you think it would be like to be all alone with some really hungry lions?
6. How would you feel if someone tricked you into doing something mean to your best friend?
7. What can we learn from Daniel's experience?

DISCOVERING PRAYER

Snack time can be a great time to teach preschoolers about prayer. You can also take prayer requests, review previous prayer requests, and receive praise reports.

1. Have you ever been in a situation where you felt you needed protection?
2. When should we pray for protection?

LET'S CREATE!

Paper Plate Lion
Supplies Needed: Paper plates, yellow orange and brown paper strips, glue, marker, and crayons.
- Give each child a paper plate.
- Have them draw a lion face in the middle with a marker.
- Let the kids glue on strips of colored paper around the edge of the plate.
- Let the kids color the rest of their plate if they want to.

Lion Cookies
Supplies Needed: Paper plates, undecorated cookies, frosting, plastic knives, cake decorations.
- Give each child a cookie on a paper plate.
- Let them decorate their cookies to look like lions with the frosting and candy.

Mother's Day Card
Supplies Needed: Paper, stickers, miscellaneous craft supplies, glue, and scissors.
- Give each child a piece of paper.
- Let them create a card for their mothers.

LESSON 3: HANNAH'S PRAYER

Supplies Needed for this Lesson:

Ball	Nail	Cups or Empty Cans	Hammer	Stickers
String	Costumes	Paper	Crayons	Tape
Marker	Stapler	Jars with Lids	Old Magazines	

LET'S PLAY A GAME!

Individual Play

Sky Ball
Supplies Needed: Ball.
- Have the kids get into a circle and assign each child a number.
- Throw the ball into the air and call out a number.
- The child who has that number, gets to catch the ball.
- The child then gets to call out a number and so on.
- Explain that, just like the kids had to give up the ball to someone else, sometimes we have to give things up to God so He can take care of them.

Multiple Play

God Can Hear Me
Supplies Needed: Small nail, cups or empty cans, hammer, long string.
- Before class, prepare several "telephones" by putting a hole in the bottom of the cups or cans and connecting them with the string.
- Ask the kids how we can communicate with people who live far away that we can't see all the time.
- Explain that when we pray, we are communicating to God. Explain that God isn't far away, but we can't see Him.
- Break the kids into pairs and give them each a phone.
- Show them how the phones work and let the kids practice talking to each other in them.

MEMORY VERSE

Read the memory verse to the kids, showing them the hand motions to help them learn it. Have the kids repeat the verse with you a couple times while doing the hand motions.

Never – Hold one finger up and wiggle it back and forth.
Stop – Hold one hand out in front you.
Praying – Fold hands together in prayer.

> Copy and cut out the memory verse cards for this month so the kids can take them home to practice!

LET'S LEARN GOD'S WORD!

> **Teacher Preparation**
> Before class, choose one of the following Hands-On Activities for the kids to do while you read the story.

Acting the Part
Supplies Needed: Costumes (optional).
Let the kids dress up and act out the scenes of the story as you read it to them.

Draw Me a Picture
Supplies Needed: Crayons, markers or pencils, paper.
- Give each child a piece of paper.
- Have them draw pictures of items or people they hear about in the story as you read it to them.

Read these verses out of a children's Bible while the kids do their hands-on activity. After reading the verses, engage the kids by asking questions about the text. Below are some questions to get you started.

> **Lesson Time Verses**
> 1 Samuel 1:2-7
> 1 Samuel 1:10-18
> 1 Samuel 1:20-22

Discussion Questions

1. We've been talking about prayer all this month and how important it is. As you get older and start praying more, God will start putting things in your heart that you'll want as bad Hannah did. You'll start to pray for it all the time until God gives it to you. Do any of you know what it's like to want something so bad you can't stop thinking about it?
2. When Samuel was just a little boy she took him to live at the temple. How would you feel if your parents left you at church and you only saw them on Sundays? What do you think you would do all day if you lived at the church?
3. Hannah gave Samuel to the Lord because God had blessed Hannah with Samuel. Did you know we can give ourselves to the Lord, just like Hannah gave Samuel to the Lord? How do you think we can give ourselves to the Lord?
4. Do you think if we gave up some of our play time to pray and read the Bible that we would be giving ourselves to God?
5. Do you think it can be hard to remember to pray?
6. How can we remind ourselves to pray?

DISCOVERING PRAYER

Snack time can be a great time to teach preschoolers about prayer. You can also take prayer requests, review previous prayer requests, and receive praise reports.

1. What are some things you really want that we can pray for?
2. What are some things we can pray for other people?
3. Why do you think God wants us to pray for other people?

LET'S CREATE!

I Will Pray For...
Supplies Needed: Paper, marker, crayons.
- Before class, take several blank pieces of paper and on the top write "I will pray for..."
- Give each child one of these papers.
- Trace one of the child's hands-on the paper and let the kids decorate their hands.
- As they decorate, go around the table and have the kids come up with things to pray about.
- Write them on the fingers of the hand outline.

Prayer Journal
Supplies Needed: Several pieces of paper folded over and stapled in the middle to make a book.
- Before class, create the booklets.
- On the front write "Prayer Journal".
- Give each child a booklet.
- Have kids draw pictures on the inside of things they want to remember to pray about.
- Tell the kids they can look at their journal to remind them to pray and so they can look back and see which prayers God has answered.
- Let the kids decorate their journals.

Prayer Jar
Supplies Needed: Small jars with lids, pictures of things the kids can pray about (Old magazines work great!), stickers, and tape.
- Give each child a small jar with a lid and let the kids decorate the outside of their jars.
- Help the kids tape one of the pictures to the outside of the jar.
- Let the kids choose pictures they want to put inside their jar.
- Explain that the kids can take out a picture and pray for whatever is in the picture.
- Tell the kids they can find other pictures at home to put in their jar.

LESSON 4: PAUL IN PRISON

Supplies Needed for this Lesson:

Music	Masking Tape	Costumes	Paper
Paint Smocks	Paint Brushes	Marshmallows	Toothpicks
Paper Plates	Hole Punch	Ribbon	Beans or Rice
Stickers	Crayons	Paint	Jail Cell

LET'S PLAY A GAME!

Individual Play

Freeze Praise
Supplies Needed: Music.
- Put some praise music on.
- Have the kids dance around.
- Stop the music.
- Everyone has to freeze.
- Ask someone to shout out their favorite thing about God.
- Start the music again.
- Continue until all children have given an answer.

Multiple Play

Jail Tag
Supplies Needed: "Jail", masking tape.
- For every five children, choose one child to be a jailer.
- For every jail set up, have one child be the "earthquake".
- Everyone else will be Paul and Silas.
- Choose two corners of the room to be bases.
- Have the jailer stand in the middle of the room. You can use masking tape to create a circle for the jailer to stand in if you wish.
- When you say "go" have all the children try to run from one base to the other.
- If any of the kids get tagged, they have to go to jail.
- When the kids get to jail, the child playing the earthquake will gently shake the child and they will be free from jail. Every now and then, switch children so everyone gets the chance to be the jailer or the earthquake.

MEMORY VERSE

Read the memory verse to the kids, showing them the hand motions to help them learn it. Have the kids repeat the verse with you a couple times while doing the hand motions.

Never – Hold one finger up and wiggle it back and forth.
Stop – Hold one hand out in front you.
Praying – Fold hands together in prayer.

> Copy and cut out the memory verse cards for this month so the kids can take them home to practice!

LET'S LEARN GOD'S WORD!

Teacher Preparation
Before class, choose one of the following Hands-On Activities for the kids to do while you read the story.

Acting the Part
Supplies Needed: Costumes (optional).
- Have the kids dress up and act out the story.

Paint Me a Picture
Supplies Needed: Paper, paint, paint smocks, brushes.
- Give each child a piece of paper.
- Tell them to paint pictures of things they hear in the story.
- Let the kids paint while you read the story.
- After a paragraph or two, ask the kids what pictures they're painting from that paragraph.

Read these verses out of a children's Bible while the kids do their hands-on activity. After reading the verses, engage the kids by asking questions about the text. Below are some questions to get you started.

> **Lesson Time Verses**
> Acts 16:16-21
> Acts 16:25-28
> Acts 16:29-36

Discussion Questions

1. Did you know praise and worship, is a type of prayer?
2. Why do you think Paul and Silas didn't run away after the earthquake?
3. Why do you think God freed Paul and Silas from prison?
4. Prison is not a nice place to be, do you think it was easy for Paul and Silas to praise God while they were in prison? Why or why not?
5. Isn't it neat how God helped Paul and Silas?

DISCOVERING PRAYER

Snack time can be a great time to teach preschoolers about prayer. You can also take prayer requests, review previous prayer requests, and receive praise reports.

1. Where are some places where it might be harder to pray?
2. Sometimes when it feels hardest to pray is the best time to pray. Why do you think that is?
3. What are some things we can pray about when it's hardest to pray?

LET'S CREATE!

Marshmallow Jail
Supplies Needed: Marshmallows, toothpicks.
- Have bowls of toothpicks and marshmallows on the table.
- Show the kids how to stick the toothpicks into the marshmallows to create shapes.
- Have the kids create their own jail cell out of the toothpicks and marshmallows.

Musical Shaker
Supplies Needed: Paper plates, hole punch, ribbon, beans or rice, crayons, stickers.
- Before class, use a hole punch to punch holes evenly around the edges of paper plates.
- Give each child two paper plates with holes around the edges.
- Help the kids tie ribbons through the holes about half way around the plate.
- Let the kids put some beans inside the plates.
- Help the kids tie ribbons in the rest of the holes.
- Let the kids decorate their shaker with crayons and stickers.

LESSON 5: ELIJAH'S PRAYER & A CONTEST

Supplies Needed for this Lesson:

Green & Red Paper	Paper Bags	Crayons	Rocks
Sticks	Clear Plastic Box	Water Table	Paint
Pitcher of Water	Costumes	Toy Lamb	Markers
Battery Operated Candles	Paint Brushes	Paint Smocks	Paper Plates
Marshmallows	Stick Pretzels	Gummy Bears	Toothpicks

LET'S PLAY A GAME!

Individual Play

Flame Dancers
Supplies Needed: Green and red paper.
- Have the kids stand on one side of the room and have them act like fire.
- Explain that God sent fire to burn an offering for Elijah, but the god the other people were worshiping, didn't light their fire. This is because it wasn't a real god.
- Tell the kids that when you hold up the green paper and say "The True God" the kids or 'flames' can come toward you.
- When you hold up the red paper say "False God." The kids, or 'flames', must freeze because no fire came to their offering. If a child moves on red, they have to go back to the beginning.

Multiple Play

Fire Bags
Supplies Needed: Paper sacks colored to look like fire.
- Before class, take two or three paper bags and color them yellow and orange.
- Divide the kids up into two or three teams, depending on how many bags you created.
- The kids will need to get on the ground and blow the bags across the floor.
- They will then carry the bag to the starting line and the next child will take their turn.
- The first team to get all kids to blow the bag across the floor wins.

MEMORY VERSE

Read the memory verse to the kids, showing them the hand motions to help them learn it. Have the kids repeat the verse with you a couple times while doing the hand motions.

Never – Hold one finger up and wiggle it back and forth.
Stop – Hold one hand out in front you.
Praying – Fold hands together in prayer.

> Copy and cut out the memory verse cards for this month so the kids can take them home to practice!

LET'S LEARN GOD'S WORD!

Teacher Preparation
Before class, choose one of the following Hands-On Activities for the kids to do while you read the story.

The Contest in Action
Supplies Needed: Water table or shallow plastic bin, small clear plastic box, sticks, toy lamb, pitcher of water, battery operated candles.
- Before class, place a clear plastic box in the empty water table. Place the battery operated candles in the plastic box. Place the sticks around the candles inside and outside the plastic box. Place the toy lamb on the sticks.
- As you read the story, have the kids beg and yell for the fire to start itself.
- When it comes time for Elijah's part, pour the water around the plastic box. Have the kids kneel down, close their eyes and pray for God to send fire.
- As they are kneeling, turn the candles on.

Acting the Part
Supplies Needed: Costumes (optional).
- Have the kids dress up and act out the story as you read it.

Read these verses out of a children's Bible while the kids do their hands-on activity. After reading the verses, engage the kids by asking questions about the text. Below are some questions to get you started.

Lesson Time Verses
1 Kings 18:16-19
1 Kings 18:21-25
1 Kings 18:26-29
1 Kings 18:36-39

Discussion Questions
1. Have you ever had a contest with your friends? How did it turn out?
2. Why do you think Elijah was able to trust God so much even though he'd never seen God?
3. Why do you think the Hebrew people believed a false god could bring down fire?
4. Do you think we sometimes believe things that aren't true?
5. Do you think God can help us recognize when we've been believing things that aren't true?

DISCOVERING PRAYER

Snack time can be a great time to teach preschoolers about prayer. You can also take prayer requests, review previous prayer requests, and receive praise reports.

1. Have you ever seen a miracle?
2. Have you ever prayed for a miracle?
3. What kind of miracles can we pray for today?

LET'S CREATE!

Elijah's Altar
Supplies Needed: Marshmallows, stick pretzels, gummy bears, paper plates, toothpicks.
- Have the kids build an altar with the marshmallows and toothpicks.
- Let each child place pretzel sticks on top for the wood.
- Give each child yellow, orange and red gummy bears to use for fire.

Altar Rocks
Supplies Needed: Rocks, paint, marker.
- Before class, clean and dry several rocks.
- With a marker, write, "God is Awesome!." on all the rocks.
- Give each child a rock and let them paint it.

MAY MEMORY VERSE CARDS

1 Thessalonians 5:17
"Never stop praying."

1 Thessalonians 5:17
"Never stop praying."

1 Thessalonians 5:17
"Never stop praying."

1 Thessalonians 5:17
"Never stop praying."

1 Thessalonians 5:17
"Never stop praying."

1 Thessalonians 5:17
"Never stop praying."

1 Thessalonians 5:17
"Never stop praying."

1 Thessalonians 5:17
"Never stop praying."

JUNE
THE HOLY SPIRIT IS OUR HELPER

OVERVIEW

The Holy Spirit can be a difficult concept for kids to grasp. Through several hands-on lessons, the children will be introduced to our inward Helper.

Memory Verse

Psalm 46:10
"Be still and know that I am God."

Hand Motions

Be still
Put finger to lips.

And know
Point to head.

That I Am God
Point up.

LESSON 1: Who is the Holy Spirit?
This lesson will introduce the kids to the third part of the Godhead, the Holy Spirit. The kids will also learn where the Holy Spirit lives and how we can communicate with Him.

LESSON 2: Day of Pentecost
This lesson will explore the day of Pentecost and why God sent the Holy Spirit to us. The children will experience hearing the voice of the Holy Spirit for themselves.

LESSON 3: How the Holy Spirit Talks to Us
This lesson doesn't focus on any particular scripture. Instead, the kids will get more hands-on experience listening for the Holy Spirit.

LESSON 4: Praying in the Spirit
Praying in the Spirit can be difficult for young minds to grasp. This lesson will explore what speaking in tongues is and its purpose. The kids will also get more experience learning to hear the voice of the Holy Spirit.

LESSON 5: How the Holy Spirit Helps Us
The Holy Spirit gives us a lot of help in life. This lesson will explore how the kids can tap into the help He provides.

LESSON 1: WHO IS THE HOLY SPIRIT?

Supplies Needed for this Lesson:

String	Blindfolds	Tape	Strips of Cloth	Paper
Popsicle Sticks	Markers	Glue	Hard Boiled Eggs	Paint
Paint Brushes	Paint Smocks	String	Random Toys	

LET'S PLAY A GAME!

Individual Play
Blindfold Maze
Supplies Needed: String, blindfolds, five random items from around the room, and tape.
- Before class, tape a string maze around the room at about knee height.
- Have the string lead to five different objects in the room.
- When the game starts, blindfold the kids.
- Have them hold onto the string.
- The kids must find their way to the five objects and guess what the objects are.
- When the game is over, explain that the Holy Spirit guides us through life. Just like the string guided them through the maze.

Multiple Play
Three-Legged Race
Supplies Needed: Strips of cloth.
- Pair kids into teams of two.
- Tie a cloth around one leg of each child so they are attached to each other.
- Have the kids race from one side of the room to the other.
- Ask them if they had to work together during the race. Tell them God, Jesus, and the Holy Spirit also work as one.

MEMORY VERSE

Read the memory verse to the kids, showing them the hand motions to help them learn it. Have the kids repeat the verse with you a couple times while doing the hand motions.

Be still - Put finger to lips.
And know - Point to head.
That I Am God - Point up.

> Copy and cut out the memory verse cards for this month so the kids can take them home to practice!

LET'S LEARN GOD'S WORD!

Teacher Preparation
Before class, choose one of the following Hands-On Activities for the kids to do while you read the story.

The Incredible, Edible Egg
Supplies Needed: Hardboiled eggs.
- For this hands-on activity the egg will show God is three-in-one. Explain that we are also three-in-one.
- You can use one egg and pass it around, or give each child an egg to explore.

Hearing the Holy Spirit
Supplies Needed: None.
- This will be a way to help the kids practice listening for God's voice.
- Have the kids sit in a circle.
- Tell them the Holy Spirit is the one who lives in our hearts and tells us what is right from wrong. Tell the kids it takes practice, but they can learn to hear the voice of the Holy Spirit.
- Have the kids close their eyes and be very quiet.
- Tell the kids you are going to pray a short prayer. You are going to ask the Holy Spirit to give them a picture in their minds of what He is like.
- Once all the kids have their eyes closed and are quiet, pray "Holy Spirit, I pray you would give each child here a picture in their minds of what You are like."
- After a few seconds, ask the kids if anyone got a picture in their minds.
- Let the kids share their pictures. Explain that often God talks to us in pictures and dreams.

Discussion Questions

1. Who is the Holy Spirit and how does He speak to us?
2. How do we learn to hear His voice?
3. How is God the Father different from Jesus?
4. How is Jesus different from the Holy Spirit?
5. If God is three parts, and we're three parts, what are our three parts?
6. Who lives inside of us, Jesus or the Holy Spirit?
7. If Jesus doesn't live inside of us, where does He live?
8. Some of you got pictures in your mind earlier when we prayed for the Holy Spirit to give you a picture. Did you know that was the Holy Spirit talking to you?
9. Is it exciting to know God can talk to you like that?

DISCOVERING PRAYER

Snack time can be a great time to teach preschoolers about prayer. You can also take prayer requests, review previous prayer requests, and receive praise reports.

1. Do you think it's important to learn how to hear God's voice?
2. Do you think prayer is all about talking to God, or is it about hearing from God too?
3. Does anyone want to pray for the class that we can all learn to hear God's voice?

LET'S CREATE!

Trinity Craft
Supplies Needed: Popsicle sticks, markers, glue, string.
- Give each child three Popsicle sticks.
- Let the kids color their sticks with markers.
- Help the kids glue their sticks into a triangle.
- On one stick write "God the Father".
- On another write "Jesus".
- On the third write "Holy Spirit".
- Help the kids tie a piece of string through the triangle so they can hang it up.

Paint a Picture
Supplies Needed: Paper, paint, paint smocks, brushes.
- Give each child a piece of paper.
- Ask the kids to paint a picture. They can make a picture of what they think the Holy Spirit is like, or something that has three parts.
- Ideas could be an apple or other fruit with skin, flesh and seeds, a person, a triangle, etc. Or they could try to paint the picture the Holy Spirit gave them in class.

LESSON 2: THE DAY OF PENTECOST

Supplies Needed for this Lesson:

Cups	Pebbles	Rice	Water	Balloons
Costumes	Paper	Crayons	Glue	

Orange, Red & Yellow Tissue Paper

LET'S PLAY A GAME!

Individual Play

Fill it up
Supplies Needed: Cups, pebbles, rice, water.
- Give each child a cup.
- Place bowls of pebbles and rice on the table.
- Tell the kids to fill their cups up so there is no more room to put anything in it.
- When the kids finish ask them if they're sure nothing else can fit in the cup.
- Give each child a little bit of water.
- Ask them if they can fit the water into their cup.
- Have the kids pour the water into their cup and make it truly full.
- Explain that sometimes it feels like we don't have any time for God. But even when we're super busy we can find ways to fit God in. Just like the water can fill up all the empty spaces in our cups.

Multiple Play

Filled with the Holy Spirit
Supplies: Balloons.
- Give each child a balloon.
- Have the kids try to blow their balloons up. The first one to do it wins.

MEMORY VERSE

Read the memory verse to the kids, showing them the hand motions to help them learn it. Have the kids repeat the verse with you a couple times while doing the hand motions.

Be still - Put finger to lips.
And know - Point to head.
That I Am God - Point up.

> Copy and cut out the memory verse cards for this month so the kids can take them home to practice!

LET'S LEARN GOD'S WORD!

> **Teacher Preparation**
> Before class, choose one of the following Hands-On Activities for the kids to do while you read the story.

Hearing the Holy Spirit
Supplies Needed: None.
- This will be a way to help the kids practice listening for God's voice.
- Have the kids sit in a circle.
- Tell them the Holy Spirit is who lives in our hearts and tells us right from wrong.
- Tell them it takes practice, but they can learn to hear the Holy Spirit.
- Have the kids close their eyes and be very quiet.
- Tell the kids you are going to pray a short prayer. Ask the Holy Spirit to tell the kids how He feels about them.
- Once all the kids have their eyes closed and are being quiet, pray "Holy Spirit, I pray you would tell each child how you feel about them today."
- After a few seconds, ask the kids if anyone felt the Holy Spirit speak to them.
- Let the kids share. Explain that often God talks to us by giving us a feeling or emotion.

Acting the Part
Supplies Needed: Costumes (optional).
- Have the kids act out the story as you read it.

Read these verses out of a children's Bible while the kids do their hands-on activity. After reading the verses, engage the kids by asking questions about the text. Below are some questions to get you started

Lesson Time Verses
Acts 2:1-4
Acts 2:6-12
Acts 2:14, 22-24
Acts 2:32-33, 37
Acts 2:38-39

Discussion Questions

1. What day did God send the Holy Spirit to us?
2. What did the believers see when the Holy Spirit came on them?
3. Why did God send the Holy Spirit to us?
4. What do you think it would have been like if we had been there on the day of Pentecost?
5. Do you think the Holy Spirit was excited to come live on the inside of us?

DISCOVERING PRAYER

Snack time can be a great time to teach preschoolers about prayer. You can also take prayer requests, review previous prayer requests, and receive praise reports.

1. Speaking in tongues is kind of like speaking another language, except it's God's language. Would any of you like to speak in tongues?

NOTE: If any children express an interest in receiving the baptism of the Holy Spirit you can lead them in the following short prayer. After the prayer, encourage the kids to begin praying. Pray in tongues with them. If you or your teachers do not feel comfortable doing this, simply let the parents know their child has shown interest in learning more about it.

"Dear Lord, thank you for sending Jesus to save us. Thank you for sending the Holy Spirit to help us. Lord I want to be baptized in the Holy Spirit. Thank you for this gift."

LET'S CREATE!

Holy Spirit Fire
Supplies Needed: Paper, orange, yellow and red tissue paper, glue.
- Give each child a piece of paper.
- Let the kids tear up pieces of tissue paper and glue them to the paper to make flames.

Draw Me a Picture
Supplies Needed: Paper, crayons.
- Give each child a piece of paper. Have them draw pictures of what they heard or learned from the lesson.

LESSON 3: HOW THE HOLY SPIRIT TALKS TO US

Supplies Needed for this Lesson:

Crayons	Paper	Watery Paint	Straws	Toothpicks
Paint Smocks	Stickers	Misc. Craft Supplies	Scissors	Glue

LET'S PLAY A GAME!

Individual Play

Holy Spirit Says
Supplies Needed: None.
- This game is played just like "Simon Says".
- Instead of saying "Simon Says", you'll say "The Holy Spirit says".
- If you don't say "The Holy Spirit says" before you give a command and the children follow it, they're out.

Multiple Play

Telephone
Supplies Needed: None.
- Have the kids sit in a circle with you.
- Tell the kids you're going to give the child next to you a message. That child is going to pass the message to the next person and so on.
- Tell the kids they can only whisper the message once. The person receiving the message must pass on what they think they heard. They cannot ask for the message to be repeated.
- When the message has gone around the circle, ask the kids to repeat it.
- Explain that unless we can hear someone clearly, we don't always get the correct message.
- Explain that we need to learn to hear God's voice clearly so we get the right message.

MEMORY VERSE

Read the memory verse to the kids, showing them the hand motions to help them learn it. Have the kids repeat the verse with you a couple times while doing the hand motions.

Be still - Put finger to lips.
And know - Point to head.
That I Am God - Point up.

> Copy and cut out the memory verse cards for this month so the kids can take them home to practice!

LET'S LEARN GOD'S WORD!

> ### Teacher Preparation
> Before class, choose one of the following Hands-On Activities for the kids to do while you read the story.

Hearing the Holy Spirit
Supplies Needed: None.
- This will help the kids practice listening for God's voice.
- Have the kids sit in a circle and explain that the Holy Spirit is who lives in our hearts and tells us right from wrong.
- Tell the kids it takes practice, but they can learn to hear the voice of the Holy Spirit.
- Have the kids close their eyes and be very quiet.
- Tell the kids you are going to pray a short prayer. Ask the Holy Spirit to give them a picture of an animal or something in nature that represents what He is like.
- Once all the kids have their eyes closed and are quiet, pray "Holy Spirit, I pray you would give each child here a picture of an animal or something in nature that will remind them of what You are like."
- After a few seconds, ask the kids if anyone got a picture in their minds.
- Let the kids share their pictures and explain that often God talks to us in pictures and dreams.

Who am I?
Supplies Needed: None.
- Have the kids sit in a circle.
- Tell them people can have different ideas of what God the Father, Jesus and the Holy Spirit are like.
- Tell the kids we're going to pray and ask God to show us who He really is.
- Explain that we won't take a lot of time, but they do need to sit still and be quiet so everyone can focus.
- Have the kids close their eyes.
- Have the kids repeat after you as you pray, "Father God, please give us a picture in our minds of who you are, so we can know you better."
- After a few seconds, ask the kids if anyone got a picture of God the Father.
- Let the kids share their pictures.
- Repeat the process and prayer, only changing "Father God" to "Jesus" and "Holy Spirit".
- Explain to the kids that asking God to show us a picture in our minds, is one way God talks to us. Congratulate the kids for hearing God's voice.

LET'S LEARN GOD'S WORD!

Discussion Questions

2. Do you remember what we learned last week about the day of Pentecost?
3. Since we've started learning about the Holy Spirit, does it feel like you have a new friend that you can talk to?
4. Has God been speaking to any of you in dreams or pictures over the past few weeks? If so, would you like to share them?
5. Who are the three parts of God?
6. What are the three parts of us?
7. We had to sit still and be quite today, was that hard to do? Do you think it's worth it to be able to hear God's voice?
8. Do you think we can hear God's voice when we're not being quiet?

DISCOVERING PRAYER

Snack time can be a great time to teach preschoolers about prayer. You can also take prayer requests, review previous prayer requests, and receive praise reports.

1. What kinds of things can we ask the Holy Spirit to help us with?
2. Does anyone want to receive God's special language of speaking in tongues?

NOTE: If any children express an interest in receiving the baptism of the Holy Spirit you can lead them in the following short prayer. After the prayer, encourage the kids to begin praying. Pray in tongues with them. If you or your teachers do not feel comfortable doing this, simply let the parents know their child has shown interest in learning more about it.

"Dear Lord, thank you for sending Jesus to save us. Thank you for sending the Holy Spirit to help us. Lord I want to be baptized in the Holy Spirit. Thank you for this gift."

LET'S CREATE!

Draw a Picture
Supplies Needed: Crayons, paper.
- Give each child a blank piece of paper.
- Tell the kids to draw pictures of things they want to remember to pray about.
- You can also have kids draw a picture of the image God put in their mind about who He is.

LET'S CREATE!

Flame Blowers
Supplies Needed: Watery paint, straws for older kids, toothpicks for younger kids, paper, and paint smocks.
- Give each child a piece of paper.
- Tell the kids that the Holy Spirit is like fire.
- Have the kids paint a picture of fire using their straws.
- Show the kids how to put paint on their paper by dipping their straws into paint, and dropping the paint on their paper.
- Show the kids how they can blow through the straw to move the paint around.
- If anyone tries to suck up the paint instead of blowing, give them toothpicks, or cut a hole in their straw near the top.

Father's Day Cards
Supplies Needed: Paper, stickers, crayons, miscellaneous craft supplies, glue, and scissors.
- Have the kids create a Father's Day card for their fathers.

LESSON 4: PRAYING IN THE SPIRIT

Supplies Needed for this Lesson:

String	Blindfolds	Tape	Strips of Cloth	Paper
Crayons	Paint Smocks	Random Toys	Paint Brushes	Paint

LET'S PLAY A GAME!

Individual Play
Blindfold Maze
Supplies Needed: String, blindfolds, five random items from around the room, and tape.
- Before class, tape a string maze around the room at about knee height.
- Have the string lead to five different objects in the room.
- When the game starts, blindfold the kids.
- Have them hold onto the string.
- The kids must find their way to the five objects and guess what the objects are.
- When the game is over, explain that the Holy Spirit guides us through life. just like the string guided them through the maze.

Multiple Play
Three-Legged Race
Supplies Needed: Strips of cloth.
- Pair kids into teams of two.
- Tie a cloth around one leg of each child, so they are attached to each other.
- Have the kids race from one side of the room to the other.
- Explain that just like they worked together during the race, God, Jesus and the Holy Spirit work as one.

MEMORY VERSE

Read the memory verse to the kids, showing them the hand motions to help them learn it. Have the kids repeat the verse with you a couple times while doing the hand motions.

Be still - Put finger to lips.
And know - Point to head.
That I Am God - Point up.

> Copy and cut out the memory verse cards for this month so the kids can take them home to practice!

LET'S LEARN GOD'S WORD!

> **Teacher Preparation**
> Before class, choose one of the following Hands-On Activities for the kids to do while you read the story.

Who am I?
Supplies Needed: None.
- Have the kids sit in a circle.
- Tell them we can have a wrong picture of who God the Father, Jesus and the Holy Spirit really are.
- Tell the kids we're going to pray and ask God to show us how He feels about us.
- Explain that we won't take a lot of time, but the kids do need to sit still and be quiet so everyone can focus.
- Have the kids close their eyes.
- Have the kids repeat after you as you pray, "Father God, please give us a picture in our minds of how you feel about us, so we can know you better."
- After a few seconds, ask the kids if anyone got a picture.
- Let the kids share their pictures.
- Repeat the process and prayer, only changing "Father God" to "Jesus" and "Holy Spirit".
- Explain to the kids that asking God to show us a picture in our minds, is one way God talks to us. Congratulate the kids for hearing God's voice.

Hearing the Holy Spirit
Supplies Needed: None.
- This will help the kids practice listening for God's voice.
- Have the kids sit in a circle. Explain that the Holy Spirit is who lives in our hearts and tells us right from wrong.
- Tell the kids it takes practice, but they can learn to hear the voice of the Holy Spirit.
- Have the kids close their eyes and be very quiet. If any of the kids have received the baptism of the Holy Spirit, you can have them practice praying in tongues at this point.
- Tell the kids you are going to pray and ask the Holy Spirit to touch them in some way. Explain to the kids that this won't be like a friend tapping them on the shoulder, but it might be an emotion.
- Once all the kids have their eyes closed and are quiet, pray "Holy Spirit, I pray you would give each child here a touch from You."
- After a few seconds, ask the kids if anyone got anything and if they want to share.

LET'S LEARN GOD'S WORD!

Discussion Questions

1. Can you name some things that come in three parts?
2. Why do you think there are so many things that come in three parts?
3. What part of us does the Holy Spirit talk to?
4. Remember our blindfold maze? Was it frustrating not being able to see where you were going?
5. Do you think it can be hard to follow God's direction when we can't see where He's leading us?
6. Remember our Three-Legged Race game? Was it hard to figure out how to walk with your partner?
7. What do you think happens when your body, mind and spirit don't work together?
8. What do you think would happen if Jesus, God and the Holy Spirit didn't work together?
9. What do you think about praying in tongues? Is it weird?
10. Those of you that have received God's language, have you been practicing?
11. How does it make you feel when you speak in tongues?

DISCOVERING PRAYER

Snack time can be a great time to teach preschoolers about prayer. You can also take prayer requests, review previous prayer requests, and receive praise reports.

1. Today we had God show us how He feels about us. What other things can we ask God to show us?
2. Does anyone want to receive God's language and speak in tongues?

NOTE: If any children express an interest in receiving the baptism of the Holy Spirit you can lead them in the following short prayer. After the prayer, encourage the kids to begin praying. Pray in tongues with them. If you or your teachers do not feel comfortable doing this, simply let the parents know their child has shown interest in learning more about it.

"Dear Lord, thank you for sending Jesus to save us. Thank you for sending the Holy Spirit to help us. Lord I want to be baptized in the Holy Spirit. Thank you for this gift."

LET'S CREATE!

Paint a Picture
Supplies Needed: Paper, paint, paint smocks, brushes.
- Give each child a piece of paper.
- Ask them to paint a picture that will help them remember to listen for God's voice.

Draw a Picture
Supplies Needed: Paper, crayons.
- Give each child a piece of paper.
- Have them draw the picture God gave them during the lesson.

LESSON 5: HOW THE HOLY SPIRIT HELPS US

Supplies Needed for this Lesson:

String	Blindfolds	Tape	Strips of Cloth	Paper
Crayons	Paint Smocks	Paint	Paint Brushes	Glue
Empty Water Bottles		Glitter	Water	

LET'S PLAY A GAME!!

Individual Play
Holy Spirit Says
Supplies Needed: None.
- Play this game like "Simon Says".
- Instead of saying "Simon Says", you'll say "The Holy Spirit says".
- If you don't say "The Holy Spirit says" before you give a command and the children follow the command, they are out.

Multiple Play
Telephone
Supplies Needed: None.
- Have the kids sit in a circle with you.
- Tell the kids you're going to give the child next to you a message. That child is going to pass the message to the next person and so on.
- Tell the kids they can only whisper the message once. The person receiving the message must pass on what they think they hear. They cannot ask for the message to be repeated.
- When the message has gone around the circle, ask the kids to repeat the message.
- Explain that unless we can hear someone clearly, we don't get the correct message.
- Explain that we need to learn to hear God's voice clearly so we get the right message.

MEMORY VERSE

Read the memory verse to the kids, showing them the hand motions to help them learn it. Have the kids repeat the verse with you a couple times while doing the hand motions.

Be still - Put finger to lips.
And know - Point to head.
That I Am God - Point up.

> Copy and cut out the memory verse cards for this month so the kids can take them home to practice!

LET'S LEARN GOD'S WORD!

> **Teacher Preparation**
> Before class, choose one of the following Hands-On Activities for the kids to do while you read the story.

Hearing the Holy Spirit
Supplies Needed: None.
- This will be a way to help the kids practice listening for God's voice.
- Have the kids sit in a circle. Explain that the Holy Spirit is who lives in our hearts and tells us right from wrong.
- Tell the kids it takes practice, but they can learn to hear the voice of the Holy Spirit.
- Have the kids close their eyes and be very quiet. Tell the kids you are going to pray and ask the Holy Spirit to give the kids a picture in their minds of what He is like.
- Once all the kids have their eyes closed and are quiet, pray "Holy Spirit, I pray you would give each child here a picture in their minds of what You are like."
- After a few seconds, ask the kids if anyone got a picture in their minds.
- Let the kids share their pictures. Explain that often God talks to us in pictures and dreams.

Putting it into Practice
Supplies Needed: None.
- Read the following scenarios to the kids. Ask them if what happened was the right thing to do or the wrong thing. If they aren't sure of the right answer, have the kids pray and ask God to help them.

Scenario 1: Another child knocks down your block tower. Later the child who knocked your block tower down, builds their own block tower. You decide to knock it over since they knocked yours over.

Scenario 2: Dad tells you to clean up your room. You are having fun playing, but you know it's good to listen to your dad, so you stop playing and clean your room.

Scenario 3: You are at the park and you see another child fall down and hurt their knee. They start to cry. You go up to the child and ask if they are ok. The child asks you to go get her mom, but you don't know who her mom is and you're not supposed to talk to strangers. The girl points to a lady who is talking to another lady. You decide to go and tell the lady about the hurt child.

Scenario 4: Another child is playing with a toy that you want to play with. You go up to the child and take it from them.

LET'S LEARN GOD'S WORD!

Discussion Questions

1. Is it hard to do the right thing sometimes? Why do you think that is?
2. What are some ways we can remind ourselves to pray and ask the Holy Spirit for help?
3. What are the three parts of God? What are our three parts?
4. What are some ways we've found that the Holy Spirit talks to us?

DISCOVERING PRAYER

Snack time can be a great time to teach preschoolers about prayer. You can also take prayer requests, review previous prayer requests, and receive praise reports.

1. Does anyone want to receive God's language and speak in tongues?

NOTE: If any children express an interest in receiving the baptism of the Holy Spirit you can lead them in the following short prayer. After the prayer, encourage the kids to begin praying. Pray in tongues with them. If you or your teachers do not feel comfortable doing this, simply let the parents know their child has shown interest in learning more about it.

"Dear Lord, thank you for sending Jesus to save us. Thank you for sending the Holy Spirit to help us. Lord I want to be baptized in the Holy Spirit. Thank you for this gift."

LET'S CREATE!

Prayer Timer
Supplies Needed: Empty water bottles, glitter, glue, water.
- Give each child an empty water bottle and let the kids choose the color of glitter they want. Help the kids pour a good amount of glitter into their bottles.
- Fill the bottles with water. Dry off the top of the bottle and the cap.
- Put glue around the edges of the cap and twist it onto the bottle.
- Tell the kids this bottle can remind them to pray every day. Show the kids they can shake the bottle up and pray until all the glitter has settled back to the bottom.

Draw a Picture
Supplies Needed: Crayons, paper.
- Give each child a blank piece of paper.
- Tell the kids to draw pictures of things God can help them with.

JUNE MEMORY VERSE CARDS

Psalm 46:10
"Be still and know that I am God."

Psalm 46:10
"Be still and know that I am God."

Psalm 46:10
"Be still and know that I am God."

Psalm 46:10
"Be still and know that I am God."

Psalm 46:10
"Be still and know that I am God."

Psalm 46:10
"Be still and know that I am God."

Psalm 46:10
"Be still and know that I am God."

Psalm 46:10
"Be still and know that I am God."

JULY
FREEDOM IN CHRIST

OVERVIEW

Jesus paid a price to set us free, but what have we been set free from and what does that look like to a child? These lessons will explore that and more as they also explore what freedom is, how we get it, and how we can help others be free too. **This will include ideas for service projects the kids can do.**

Memory Verse

Romans 8:2
"Because of Jesus I am free from the law of sin and death."

Hand Motions

Because of Jesus
Point up.

I am free
Cross wrists and pull apart.

From the law
Hammering motion.

Of sin and death
Hold both hands in front of you, one palm up, one down. Flip them over. The palm facing down, is now up, the palm facing up is now down.

LESSON 1: What is Freedom?
Freedom can mean many things, especially to a Christ follower. This lesson will explain the basic concept of freedom versus being held captive. It will cover Peters escape from prison in Acts 12.

LESSON 2: Freedom isn't Free
This lesson will focus on serving others, specifically those who are in the military. The kids will learn what a soldier's job is and why it's so important.

LESSON 3: Freedom from Sin
It can be difficult for kids to understand that selfishness, mean words and the like are sin. This lesson will explore how we can get stuck in sin and how God helps us be free from that sin.

LESSON 4: What Does Freedom in Christ Look Like?
This lesson will compare how someone in the military protects our freedoms compared to how God sets us free.

LESSON 5: Helping Others be Free
This lesson will be a review of the month. If you have any service projects going on, this would be a great time to let the kids help put care packages together. More service projects will be available for the kids to do as well.

LESSON 1: WHAT IS FREEDOM?

Supplies Needed for this Lesson:

Small Flags	Jail Cell	Crayons	Paper	Paint
Paint Smocks	Pom-Poms	Tissues	Q-Tips	Sponges
Glitter	Salt	Glue	Costumes	
Food Coloring	Construction Paper			

LET'S PLAY A GAME!

Individual Play
Hide & Seek
Supplies Needed: None.
- Let the kids play a game of Hide and Seek.
- Explain that sometimes when we do things that aren't right we try to hide. God will always seek us out because He has set us free and wants us to know He's not mad at us.

Multiple Play
Capture the Flag
Supplies Needed: Two flags.
- Divide the kids into two teams.
- Give each team a flag.
- Have each team find a place to hide their flag.
- Make sure the other team isn't peeking.
- Once both flags are hidden, tell the kids they need to go and find the other teams flag.
- The first team to find a flag wins.

MEMORY VERSE

Read the memory verse to the kids, showing them the hand motions to help them learn it. Have the kids repeat the verse with you a couple times while doing the hand motions.

Because of Jesus – Point up.
I am free – Cross wrists and pull apart.
From the law – Hammering motion.
Of sin and death – Hold hands in front of you, one palm up, one down. Flip them over. The palm facing down is now up, the palm facing up is now down.

> Copy and cut out the memory verse cards for this month so the kids can take them home to practice!

LET'S LEARN GOD'S WORD!

> ### Teacher Preparation
> Before class, choose one of the following Hands-On Activities for the kids to do while you read the story.

Jail Time
Supplies Needed: Jail cell.
- Before class set up a jail. This can be a rope attached to the wall that the kids get under, a big box, or paper chains hung from a doorway. More ideas can be found in the reference section on page 234.
- Have the kids get into the jail.
- Ask them if they are free right now.
- Tell the kids you're going to ask them some questions.
- When they answer the questions correctly they can get out of jail and be free.

What is the memory verse? **(Because of Jesus I am free from the law of sin and death.)**

If there were no rules and you could do whatever you wanted, would you be free? **(No.)**

What did Jesus free us from? **(Sin.)**

What was the first sin? **(Disobeying God, eating the fruit.)**

How did Jesus free us from sin? **(Died on the cross.)**

What holiday will we celebrate this month? **(4th of July, Independence day.)**

When you are in timeout, how do you get out of it? **(Listen, say sorry, obey.)**

How do you get free from our classroom? **(Parent has to pick them up.)**

What is a classroom rule? **(No hitting, be kind to each other, no stealing, share toys etc.)**

Who is your favorite teacher in the whole world? **(Hopefully your name!** ☺ **)**

Cards from Home
Supplies Needed: Paper, crayons.
- Give each child a piece of paper folded in half.
- Let them create a card for a soldier while the story is being read.

Acting the Part
Supplies Needed: Costumes (optional).
- Have the kids act out the story as you read it.

LET'S LEARN GOD'S WORD!

Read these verses out of a children's Bible while the kids do their hands-on activity. After reading the verses, engage the kids by asking questions about the text. Below are some questions to get you started.

Lesson Time Verses	
Acts 12:1-5	Acts 12:12-15
Acts 12:6-8	Acts 12:16-18
Acts 12:9-11	

Discussion Questions

2. Was Peter free when he was in jail?
3. Are there other ways, besides jail, that makes us not free? What are they?
4. Did you know sin can make us not free? How do you think that's possible?
5. What did you think of our story today? Were there any funny parts in it?
6. What did you think about our Hide and Seek game today? Have you ever done something you knew was wrong and then tried to hide it? Sometimes we hide when we do wrong, but what do we need to do when we do wrong?
7. Do you think we are free if we do something wrong and don't tell anyone about it?
8. Would you worry all the time if you were trying to keep people from finding out about something you'd done?
9. Do you think you would feel good on the inside if you were always worrying?

DISCOVERING PRAYER

Snack time can be a great time to teach preschoolers about prayer. You can also take prayer requests, review previous prayer requests, and receive praise reports.

1. Would anyone like to pray and thank God for freeing us from sin and death?
2. What other freedoms can we thank God for?

LET'S CREATE!

Fireworks
Supplies Needed: Black construction paper, glue, glitter OR salt and food coloring.
- Give each child a piece of black paper. Let them draw fireworks with the glue.
- Let them sprinkle glitter on the glue.
- You can also let the kids sprinkle salt on their glue. Let them squeeze drops of food coloring onto the salt and watch it spread!

LET'S CREATE!

What Makes a Firework?
Supplies Needed: Paper, paint, pom-poms, paint smocks, sponges, tissues, Q-tips, miscellaneous items to explore with paint.
- Give each child a piece of paper.
- Set up bowls of paint.
- Let the kids create fireworks by exploring different tools to dip into the paint.

LESSON 2: FREEDOM ISN'T FREE

Supplies Needed for this Lesson:

| Jail Cell | Paper | Crayons | Scissors | Glue | Stickers |
| Marker | Cardstock | Baggies | Paint | Sponges | Paint Smocks |

LET'S PLAY A GAME!

Individual Play
Hide & Seek
Supplies Needed: None.
- Let the kids play a game of Hide and Seek.
- Explain that sometimes when we do things that aren't right, we try to hide. God will always seek us out because He has set us free and wants us to know He's not mad at us.

Multiple Play
Freeze Tag
Supplies Needed: None.
- Let the kids play a game of freeze tag.
- Explain to the children, freedom always comes with a price, just like some of them got tagged while they were trying to free a friend.

MEMORY VERSE

Read the memory verse to the kids, showing them the hand motions to help them learn it. Have the kids repeat the verse with you a couple times while doing the hand motions.

Because of Jesus – Point up.
I am free – Cross wrists and pull apart.
From the law – Hammering motion.
Of sin and death – Hold hands in front of you, one palm up, one down. Flip them over. The palm facing down is now up, the palm facing up is now down.

> Copy and cut out the memory verse cards for this month so the kids can take them home to practice!

LET'S LEARN GOD'S WORD!

Teacher Preparation
Before class, choose one of the following Hands-On Activities for the kids to do while you read the story.

What Soldiers Do
Supplies Needed: Jail cell.
- Have one or two kids stand in the jail. For information on how to create a jail cell, please see the reference section on page 234.
- Have one or two kids be guards at the jail.
- Have the rest of the kids fight a pretend battle to free the prisoners.
- Remind the kids not to really hit each other, only pretend.

Cards for Soldiers
Supplies Needed: Paper, scissors, glue, stickers, marker.
- Help the kids fold a piece of paper in half.
- Ask them what they would like to write on their cards and help them write it.
- Let the kids decorate their cards.

Discussion Questions

1. Do any of you have family in the military?
2. Did you know people in the military have to leave their families for a long time?
3. Would it make you sad if one of your parents missed your next two birthdays?
4. Do you think people in the military miss their families?
5. Do you think they like to get cards from people, thanking them for what they're doing?
6. What can we do for families who are waiting for their loved ones to come home?
7. Do you think they might need hugs sometimes?
8. We talked about serving others in class. People in the military serve everyone in America by keeping us safe. Is making cards for them a way to serve them?
9. What ways can we serve our family and friends?
10. Soldiers help us stay safe and free in America, but who else set us free?
11. How did Jesus set us free?
12. What did Jesus set us free from?

DISCOVERING PRAYER

Snack time can be a great time to teach preschoolers about prayer. You can also take prayer requests, review previous prayer requests, and receive praise reports.

1. Soldiers do a lot to keep us safe. Do you think it's important to pray for them?
2. Who else can we pray for?

LET'S CREATE!

Medals of Love
Supplies Needed: Copies of medals on cardstock from page 135, crayons, scissors, and baggies.
- Give each child a copy of a page of medals.
- Have the kids color the medals.
- Help the kids cut out their medals.
- Tell the kids they are to give the medals to people they are thankful to have in their lives.

My Sins are Washed Away
Supplies Needed: Paint, sponges cut out in shapes, marker, paper, paint smocks.
- Before class, write on several pieces of paper, "My sins are washed away."
- Give each child a paper.
- Have several bowls of paint on the table.
- Let the kids dip the sponges into the paint and decorate their papers.

1 Year of Sunday School Lessons for 3-5 year olds | Angela E. Powell

MEDALS OF LOVE

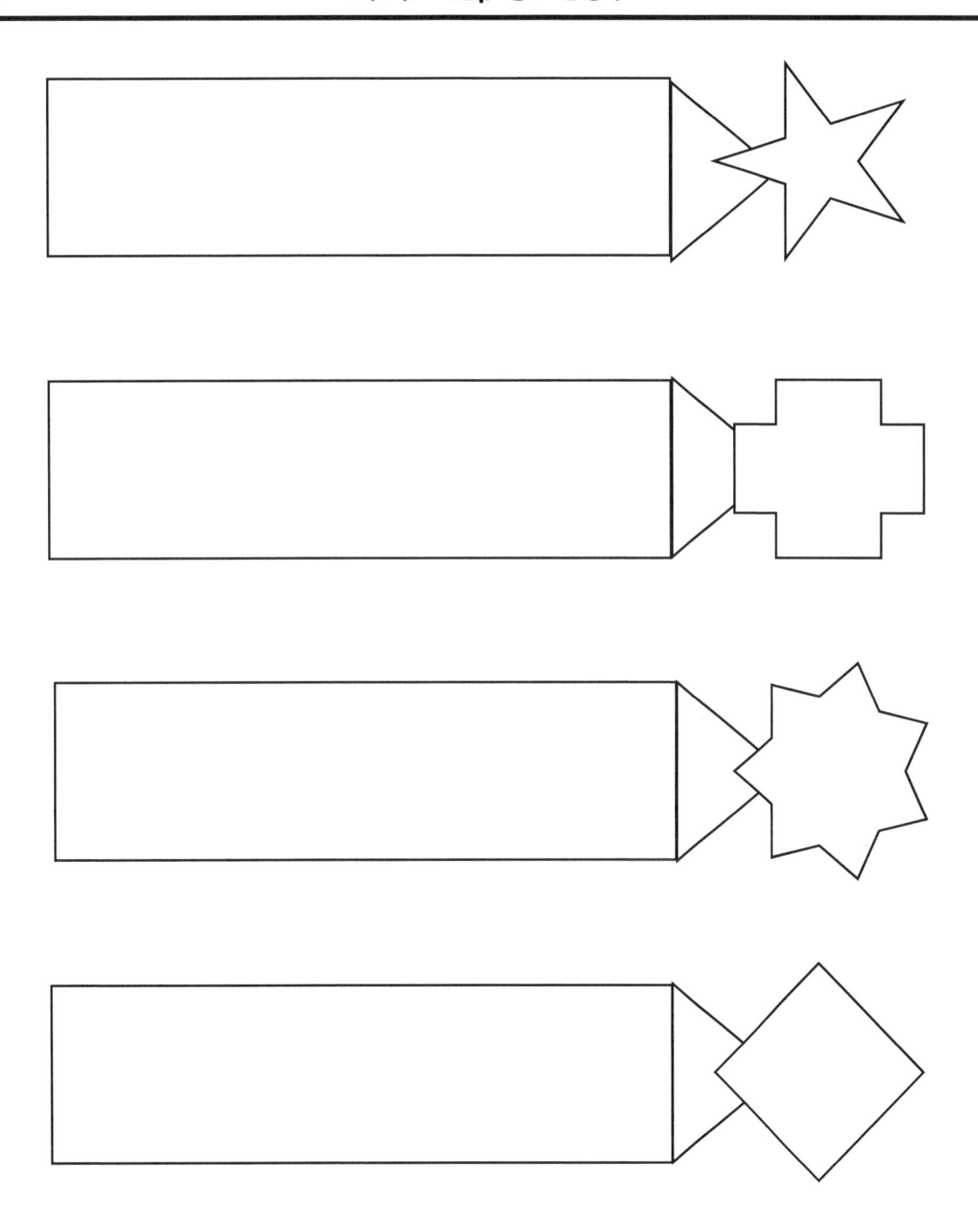

135

LESSON 3: FREEDOM FROM SIN

Supplies Needed for this Lesson:
Flags   Painter's Tape   String or Strips of Cloth   Paper
Paint   Paint Brushes   Paint Smocks   Crayons
Small Puppets or Stuffed Animals

LET'S PLAY A GAME!

Individual Play
Hide & Seek
Supplies Needed: None.
- Let the kids play a game of Hide and Seek.
- Explain that sometimes when we do things that aren't right, we try to hide. God will always seek us out because He has set us free and wants us to know He's not mad at us.

Multiple Play
Capture the Flag
Supplies Needed: Two flags.
- Divide the kids into two teams.
- Give each team a flag.
- Have each team find a place to hide their flag.
- Make sure the other team isn't peeking.
- Once both flags are hidden, tell the kids they need to go and find the other teams flag.
- The first team to find a flag wins.

MEMORY VERSE

Read the memory verse to the kids, showing them the hand motions to help them learn it. Have the kids repeat the verse with you a couple times, while doing the hand motions.

Because of Jesus – Point up.
I am free – Cross wrists and pull apart.
From the law – Hammering motion.
Of sin and death – Hold hands in front of you, one palm up, one down. Flip them over. The palm facing down is now up, the palm facing up is now down.

> Copy and cut out the memory verse cards for this month so the kids can take them home to practice!

LET'S LEARN GOD'S WORD!

Teacher Preparation
Before class, choose one of the following Hands-On Activities for the kids to do while you read the story.

The Garden of Eden
Supplies Needed: None.
- Ask the kids what they think it would have been like to live in the Garden of Eden before there was sin.
- Explain that there was no such thing as fear or sadness.
- Ask the kids if they would like it if they didn't ever have to be afraid or sad ever again.
- Ask the kids what kinds of things they would do if they didn't have any fear.

All Tied Up.
Supplies Needed: Small puppets or stuffed animals, string or strips of cloth.
- Take string or strips of cloth and tie several puppets or stuffed animals onto the kids.
- Take more string or strips of cloth and tie their hands and feet together.
- Explain that the items tied to them are things like lying, cheating, stealing, disobeying parents etc.
- Have the kids try to get the items off by themselves.
- After a minute, explain that it's really hard for us to get rid of sin by ourselves.
- Ask the kids if they know who can help us get rid of sin.
- Explain that Jesus is the only one who can save us from sin and He did that when He died on the cross.
- Go to each child and ask them if they want Jesus to free them.
- When they say yes, untie their hands and feet and help them remove the objects.

Discussion Questions

1. What do you think it would have been like to live in the Garden of Eden before there was sin?
2. Do you think there was sickness in the Garden of Eden?
3. What about fear or pain?
4. Do you think you would have ever gotten bit by an animal in the Garden?
5. Why do you think it's important that we learn about freedom?
6. Do you think it's important to know and remember what Jesus did for us?
7. If you didn't know that Jesus set you free from sin, do you think it would be easy to believe you had to live with sin forever?

DISCOVERING PRAYER

Snack time can be a great time to teach preschoolers about prayer. You can also take prayer requests, review previous prayer requests, and receive praise reports.

1. What are some things we can talk about with God when we pray?
2. How can we pray when we've done something wrong?
3. When we pray, do we always have to ask God for things?
4. What are some things we can pray and thank God for today?

LET'S CREATE!

Cross Craft
Supplies Needed: Paper, paint, painter's tape, brushes.
- Before class, use painter's tape to make a cross on paper.
- Give each child a piece of paper with a cross on it.
- Let the kids paint their picture.
- When the picture is dry, take the tape off.

Draw a Picture
Supplies Needed: Paper, crayons.
- Give each child a piece of paper.
- Have them draw pictures of things they heard in the lesson.

LESSON 4: WHAT DOES FREEDOM IN CHRIST LOOK LIKE?

Supplies Needed for this Lesson:

Jail Cell	String	Strips of Cloth	Small Puppets
Stuffed Animals	Blueberries	Strawberries	String Cheese
Bowls	Toothpicks	Sugar Cookies	Plates
Plastic Knives	White Frosting	Red and Blue Sprinkles	

LET'S PLAY A GAME!

Individual Play
Hide & Seek
Supplies Needed: None.
- Let the kids play a game of Hide and Seek.
- Explain that sometimes when we do things that aren't right, we try to hide. God will always seek us out because He has set us free and wants us to know He's not mad at us.

Multiple Play
Freeze Tag
Supplies Needed: None.
- Let the kids play a game of freeze tag.
- Explain to the children, freedom always comes with a price, just like some of them got tagged while they were trying to free a friend.

MEMORY VERSE

Read the memory verse to the kids, showing them the hand motions to help them learn it. Have the kids repeat the verse with you a couple times while doing the hand motions.

Because of Jesus – Point up.
I am free – Cross wrists and pull apart.
From the law – Hammering motion.
Of sin and death – Hold hands in front of you, one palm up, one down. Flip them over. The palm facing down is now up, the palm facing up is now down.

> Copy and cut out the memory verse cards for this month so the kids can take them home to practice!

LET'S LEARN GOD'S WORD!

> ### Teacher Preparation
> Before class, choose one of the following Hands-On Activities for the kids to do while you read the story.

Jail Time
Supplies Needed: Jail cell.
- Have the kids get into the jail. For more information on how to create a jail cell, please see page 234.
- Ask them if they are free right now.
- Tell the kids you're going to ask them some questions.
- When they answer the questions correctly they can get out of jail.

What is the memory verse? **(Because of Jesus I am free from the law of sin and death.)**

If there were no rules and you could do whatever you wanted, would you be free? **(No.)**

What did Jesus free us from? **(Sin.)**

What was the first sin? **(Disobeying God, eating the fruit.)**

How did Jesus free us from sin? **(Died on the cross.)**

What holiday will we celebrate this month? **(4th of July, Independence day.)**

When you are in timeout, how to you get out of it? **(Listen, Say Sorry, Obey.)**

How do you get free from our classroom? **(Parent has to pick them up.)**

What is a classroom rule? **(No hitting, Be kind to each other, No stealing, Share toys etc.)**

Who is your favorite teacher in the whole world? **(Hopefully your name! ☺)**

All Tied Up.
Supplies Needed: Small puppets or stuffed animals, string or strips of cloth.
- Take the string or strips of cloth and tie several puppets or stuffed animals onto the kids.
- Take more string or strips of cloth and tie their hands and feet together.
- Explain that the items tied to them are things like lying, cheating, stealing, disobeying parents etc.
- Have the kids try to get the items off by themselves.
- After a minute, explain that it's really hard for us to get rid of sin by ourselves.
- Ask the kids if they know who can help us get rid of sin.
- Explain that Jesus is the only one who can save us from sin. He did that when He died on the cross.
- Go to each child and ask them if they want Jesus to free them.
- When they say yes, untie their hands and feet and help them remove the objects.

LET'S LEARN GOD'S WORD!

What Soldiers Do
Supplies Needed: Jail cell.
- Have one or two kids stand in the jail. For more information on how to create a jail cell, please see page 234.
- Have one or two kids be guards at the jail.
- Have the rest of the kids fight a pretend battle to free the prisoners.
- Remind the kids not to really hit each other, only pretend.

Discussion Questions

1. We've learned a lot this month about freedom. Can you remember some of the things we talked about?
2. What are some different ways we are free?
3. How are we free in America? Who keeps us safe?
4. How are we free in Jesus Christ?
5. What else, besides sin, does God want to set us free from?
6. If we don't learn about how to be free in Jesus, do you think we will be able to help other people find freedom in Jesus?
7. What does it look like to be free in Jesus?
8. Is there sickness if we're free in Christ? What about pain?
9. We can't always get away from these things, but if we know Jesus has given us the ability to be free, shouldn't we walk in freedom most of the time?
10. How do you walk in freedom?
11. Can you believe what the Bible says about our freedom?
12. If you feel sick, can you believe God has freed you from sickness, even though sickness is trying to get on you?
13. Do you think people who walk in freedom pray for other people?
14. The Bible says a lot about how Jesus set us free. Do you think it's important that we read our Bible and learn about those things?

DISCOVERING PRAYER

Snack time can be a great time to teach preschoolers about prayer. You can also take prayer requests, review previous prayer requests, and receive praise reports.

1. Soldiers do a lot to keep us safe. Do you think it's important that we remember to pray for them?
2. Who else do you think we can pray for?
3. Would anyone like to pray and thank God for setting us free from sin and death?
4. What other freedoms can we thank God for?

LET'S CREATE!

Craft Snack
Supplies Needed: Toothpicks, blueberries, string cheese, strawberries and bowls.
- Let the kids create firework kabobs, by putting cut strawberries, blueberries and string cheese on toothpicks.
- Let the kids create some to eat and some to take home.

July 4th Cookies
Supplies Needed: Plain cookies, white frosting, red and blue sprinkles, plates, knives.
- Give each child one or two cookies to decorate.
- Let the kids spread frosting on their cookies and put sprinkles on them.

LESSON 5: HELPING OTHERS BE FREE

Supplies Needed for this Lesson:

Flags | Jail Cell | Stuffed Animals | String
Strips of Cloth | Small Puppets | Paint | Cardstock
Paint Smocks | Crayons | Tissue Paper | Paper Plates
Scissors | Glue | Hole Punch
Different Sizes of Plastic Lids

LET'S PLAY A GAME!

Individual Play
Hide & Seek
Supplies Needed: None.
- Let the kids play a game of Hide and Seek.
- Explain that sometimes when we do things that aren't right, we try to hide. God will always seek us out because He has set us free and wants us to know He's not mad at us.

Multiple Play
Capture the Flag
Supplies Needed: Two Flags.
- Divide the kids into two teams.
- Give each team a flag.
- Have each team find a place to hide their flag.
- Make sure the other team isn't peeking.
- Once both flags are hidden, tell the kids they need to go and find the other teams flag.
- The first team to find a flag wins.

MEMORY VERSE

Read the memory verse to the kids, showing them the hand motions to help them learn it. Have the kids repeat the verse with you a couple times while doing the hand motions.

Because of Jesus – Point up.
I am free – Cross wrists and pull apart.
From the law – Hammering motion.
Of sin and death – Hold hands in front of you, one palm up, one down. Flip them over. The palm facing down is now up, the palm facing up is now down.

> Copy and cut out the memory verse cards for this month so the kids can take them home to practice!

LET'S LEARN GOD'S WORD!

> **Teacher Preparation**
> Before class, choose one of the following Hands-On Activities for the kids to do while you read the story.

What Soldiers Do
Supplies Needed: Jail cell.
- Have one or two kids stand in the jail. For more information on how to create a jail cell, please see page 234.
- Have one or two kids be guards at the jail.
- Have the rest of the kids fight a pretend battle to free the prisoners.
- Remind the kids not to really hit each other, only pretend.

All Tied Up.
Supplies Needed: Small puppets or stuffed animals, string or strips of cloth.
- Take the string or strips of cloth and tie several puppets or stuffed animals onto the kids.
- Take more string or strips of cloth and tie their hands and feet together.
- Explain that the items tied to them are things like lying, cheating, stealing, disobeying parents etc.
- Have the kids try to get the items off by themselves.
- After a minute, explain that it's really hard for us to get rid of sin by ourselves.
- Ask the kids if they know who can help us get rid of sin.
- Explain that Jesus is the only one who can save us from sin and He did that when He died on the cross.
- Go to each child and ask them if they want Jesus to free them.
- When they say yes, untie their hands and feet and help them remove the objects.

Service Projects for Military and their Families
Supplies Needed: Information about a local organization to donate items to. Some suggested organizations are listed in the reference section of this book on pages 238.
- Have the kids put together care packages, participate in creating cards for military, or sending toys to military children, etc.

LET'S LEARN GOD'S WORD!

Discussion Questions

1. What does it mean to be free?
2. What is the difference between freedom in America and freedom in Jesus?
3. Did you know that in some countries, people aren't allowed to pray to God, or dress the way they want to?
4. Do you think telling other people about what Jesus did for us will help other people be free in Jesus?

DISCOVERING PRAYER

Snack time can be a great time to teach preschoolers about prayer. You can also take prayer requests, review previous prayer requests, and receive praise reports.

1. Who can we pray for?
2. If you see someone crying what can you do to help them?
3. What kinds of things can we pray about for our brothers and sisters and parents?
4. Are there any fears you have that you would like to pray about today?

LET'S CREATE!

Paint Splatter Fireworks
Supplies Needed: Different size plastic lids, paint, cardstock and paint smocks.
- Give each child a piece of cardstock.
- Have the kids put small dots of paint close to each other on the paper.
- Place a lid over the paint and hold it down.
- Have the kid's pound on the lid and watch as the paint splatters.
- Pick up the lid and show the kids their fireworks.

God Bless America Wreath
Supplies Needed: Crayons, tissue paper, paper plates, scissors, glue, hole punch, and string.
- Before class write "God Bless America" in the center of several paper plates.
- Give each child a paper plate.
- Let the kids color their wreath.
- The kids can take red, blue and white tissue paper and glue small pieces to the plate.
- Use a hole punch at the top of the wreath.
- Tie string through the hole.

JULY MEMORY VERSE CARDS

Romans 8:2
"Because of Jesus I am free from the law of sin and death."

Romans 8:2
"Because of Jesus I am free from the law of sin and death."

Romans 8:2
"Because of Jesus I am free from the law of sin and death."

Romans 8:2
"Because of Jesus I am free from the law of sin and death."

Romans 8:2
"Because of Jesus I am free from the law of sin and death."

Romans 8:2
"Because of Jesus I am free from the law of sin and death."

Romans 8:2
"Because of Jesus I am free from the law of sin and death."

Romans 8:2
"Because of Jesus I am free from the law of sin and death."

AUGUST
GOD WANTS TO BE YOUR BEST FRIEND

OVERVIEW

Most kids know what it means to have a best friend. These lessons will teach the kids that Jesus wants to be their best friend too. The kids will discover that even though they can't see Jesus, it is still possible to be best friends with Him.

Memory Verse

Matthew 28:20
"I am with you always."

Hand Motions

I Am
Point up.

With you
Point to someone.

Always
Point up with one finger and move it in a circular motion.

LESSON 1: What is a Friend?
This lesson explores the friendship between David and Jonathan. The kids will discover what it means to be a good friend and how sometimes that can be difficult.

LESSON 2: Jesus is our BFF
The Bible has a lot to say about friendship. This lesson will explore some of the verses in the Bible that talk about Jesus being our friend and what that looks like.

LESSON 3: Zacchaeus in the Tree
Jesus was friends with people that society looked down on. This lesson will explore the case of Zacchaeus and how Jesus befriending him made a world of difference.

LESSON 4: Jesus Helps His Friends
This lesson will focus on the story of when Jesus multiplied the loaves and fish for the multitudes. The people He fed weren't Jesus' closest friends, but He still loved them and calls us to do the same.

LESSON 5: God's Friend Abraham
God called Abraham His friend. This lesson will explore the relationship God had with Abraham and how we can have the same kind of relationship with God.

LESSON 1: WHAT IS A FRIEND?

Supplies Needed for this Lesson:

| Beanbag | Chairs | Costumes | String | Beads | Ink Pad |
| Paper | Marker | Music | | | |

LET'S PLAY A GAME!

Individual Play

Beanbag Compliments

Supplies Needed: Beanbag.

- Have the kids form a circle.
- Throw the beanbag to a child and tell them something nice.
- Have the child throw the beanbag to another child and have them say something nice about that child.
- Continue until all the kids have received at least one compliment.
- Encourage the kids to say things like "you make me laugh" or "you are a good listener" etc.

Multiple Play

Cooperative Musical Chairs

Supplies Needed: Chairs, music.

- Place chairs in a line, back to back with one less chair than there are children.
- Turn the music on and have the kids walk around the chairs.
- When the music stops, the kids have to find a chair, but they must find a way for all the kids to have a seat.
- When they've accomplished this, take one chair away.
- Continue with the game until the kids can no longer figure out how to all have a seat.
- Encourage the kids to use kind words and help each other.

MEMORY VERSE

Read the memory verse to the kids, showing them the hand motions to help them learn it. Have the kids repeat the verse with you a couple times while doing the hand motions.

I Am - Point up.
With you - Point to someone.
Always - Point up with one finger and move it in a circular motion.

> Copy and cut out the memory verse cards for this month so the kids can take them home to practice!

LET'S LEARN GOD'S WORD!

Teacher Preparation
Before class, choose one of the following Hands-On Activities for the kids to do while you read the story.

Words that Hurt or Help
Supplies Needed: None.
- Ask the kids if they know what it means to be a friend.
- Tell the kids you're going to read some phrases to them. They have to decide if the words would be helpful or hurtful and explain why.

I understand.	I heard him call me a name.
I will pray for you.	You can't play with us anymore.
Your necklace is really pretty!	I don't like you.
Would you like to play with me?	Your hair is ugly.

Acting the Part
Supplies Needed: Costumes (optional).
- Let the kids act out the story as you read it.

Read these verses out of a children's Bible while the kids do their hands-on activity. After reading the verses, engage the kids by asking questions about the text. Below are some questions to get you started.

Lesson Time Verses
1 Samuel 18:1-4	1 Samuel 20:1-5
1 Samuel 18:6-9, 19:1-3	1 Samuel 20:27-30
1 Samuel 19:4-7	1 Samuel 20:35-42

Discussion Questions

1. Would it be hard to be someone's friend if your parents didn't like your friend?
2. What about if your friends mom and dad didn't like you?
3. Jonathan gave David his robe and military clothes. Do you give gifts to your friends?
4. What do you think King Saul would have done if he'd found out his son, Jonathan, was helping David escape?
5. Jonathan and David knew that because King Saul didn't like David, they wouldn't be able to see each other anymore. How would it make you feel if you could never see your best friend ever again?
6. Sometimes we lose friends because they move away. What are some other ways we might lose friends?
7. What are some ways we can keep friends?
8. What are some ways we can show love to our friends?

DISCOVERING PRAYER

Snack time can be a great time to teach preschoolers about prayer. You can also take prayer requests, review previous prayer requests, and receive praise reports.

1. What is prayer?
2. What kinds of things can we pray for our friends?

LET'S CREATE!

Friendship Bracelets
Supplies Need: String, beads.
- Give each child two pieces of string.
- Let them create two bracelets.
- Explain that one bracelet is for them to give away to a friend.

Friendship Handprints
Supplies Needed: Ink pad, plain paper, and marker.
- Before class take several pieces of plain paper and write "My friends are…" at the top of the page.
- Have the kids ask each child for their handprint.
- Write the children's names by their handprints.
- Have the kids practice asking nicely and being kind to each other.

LESSON 2: JESUS IS OUR BFF

Supplies Needed for this Lesson:

Pipe Cleaner
Crayons
Misc. Craft Supplies
Candy
Stickers
Scissors
Buttons
Paper
Beads

LET'S PLAY A GAME!

Individual Play

My Friend May I
Supplies Needed: None.
- Have all the kids stand in a line facing you.
- Let the kids take turns saying "My friend, May I…" (take 3 baby steps, 1 giant leap, etc.)
- The first one to reach you gets to take your place.
- Play until all the kids get to be at the front.

Multiple Play

Follow My Friend
Supplies Needed: None.
- Play just like "Follow the Leader".
- Let the kids take turns being the leader.

MEMORY VERSE

Read the memory verse to the kids, showing them the hand motions to help them learn it. Have the kids repeat the verse with you a couple times while doing the hand motions.

I Am - Point up.
With you - Point to someone.
Always - Point up with one finger and move it in a circular motion.

> Copy and cut out the memory verse cards for this month so the kids can take them home to practice!

LET'S LEARN GOD'S WORD!

Teacher Preparation
Before class, choose one of the following Hands-On Activities for the kids to do while you read the story.

Friendship Knot
Supplies Needed: None.
- Have the kids get in a circle, cross their arms and hold hands with two different people.
- After reading each Bible verse about God's friendship have the kids try to untangle themselves without letting go of each other's hands.
- Praise the kids for working together to solve the puzzle.

Read these verses out of a children's Bible while the kids do their hands-on activity. After reading the verses, engage the kids by asking questions about the text. Below are some questions to get you started.

Lesson Time Verses
John 15:15
Proverbs 17:17
Proverbs 22:24-25
Matthew 10:30

Discussion Questions
1. Jesus did a pretty amazing thing for us when He died on the cross didn't He?
2. What things can we do to show Jesus we want to be His best friend?
3. What kinds of things can we do to show love to other people?
4. Is it hard to show love to people all the time?
5. Is it easy to get angry sometimes?
6. What are some reasons we get angry with each other?
7. When we've been angry with a friend, how can we fix our friendship with that person?
8. Have you ever counted how many strands of hair you have?
9. It would be hard to do wouldn't it?
10. The Bible tells us God knows the number of hairs on each of our heads! That's pretty neat isn't it?

DISCOVERING PRAYER

Snack time can be a great time to teach preschoolers about prayer. You can also take prayer requests, review previous prayer requests, and receive praise reports.

1. What kinds of things can we pray about for our friends?
2. Do you think it's important to pray and ask God to help us be better friends?
3. What kinds of things can we pray about so God can help us become better friends?

LET'S CREATE!

Friendship Cards
Supplies Needed: Paper, scissors, crayons, stickers, buttons, beads, miscellaneous craft supplies.
- Let the kids create cards to give to a friend.
- Help them with any gluing or cutting.

Friendship Rings
Supplies Needed: Pipe cleaner, candy, scissors.
- Give each child two pipe cleaners.
- Have the kids make an 'X' with their pipe cleaners.
- Place a piece of candy in the center of the 'X'.
- Wrap the four pipe cleaner ends over the top of the candy and twist the ends together.
- Bend the ends into a ring.
- Twist the ends together at the top of the ring.
- Trim the ends.

LESSON 3: ZACCHAEUS IN THE TREE

Supplies Needed for this Lesson:

Music	Bags of Candy	Costumes	Paper
Scissors	Crayons	Glue	Cotton Balls
Ink Pad	Pretzel Sticks & Rods	Marshmallows	Chairs
Green Food Coloring or Sprinkles		Brown Construction Paper	

LET'S PLAY A GAME!

Individual Play
Human Statues
Supplies Needed: None.
- Tell the kids you're going to call out something and they need make their body be like that thing.
- Some things to call out can be, "Rock, bird, table, elephant, rabbit, a giving person, a loving person, etc."

Multiple Play
Musical Chairs
Supplies Needed: Chairs, music.
- Set up two rows of chairs, backs facing each other.
- Have one less chair than there are kids.
- Start the music.
- Have the kids walk around the chairs.
- When the music stops the child who doesn't have a chair is out.
- After the game, ask the kids how it felt to be out of the game.
- Ask the kids if they've ever been left out of something.
- Ask the kids if they've ever left someone else out of a game.

MEMORY VERSE

Read the memory verse to the kids, showing them the hand motions to help them learn it. Have the kids repeat the verse with you a couple times while doing the hand motions.

I Am - Point up.
With you - Point to someone.
Always - Point up with one finger and move it in a circular motion.

> Copy and cut out the memory verse cards for this month so the kids can take them home to practice!

LET'S LEARN GOD'S WORD!

Teacher Preparation
Before class, choose one of the following Hands-On Activities for the kids to do while you read the story.

Zacchaeus was a Tax Collector
Supplies Needed: Bags of candy.
- Give each child a bag of candy, but tell them they can't eat it yet.
- Have one child be Zacchaeus the Tax Collector.
- Explain that everyone has to give taxes, which is a fee we pay to the government.
- Tell the kids the tax they have to pay is two pieces of candy each.
- Explain that when Jesus was on earth, some tax collectors were bad people and would take more taxes then the people had to give.
- Have the tax collector take two candies from each child and put them in an empty bag.
- Then have the tax collector take one or two more pieces from each child's bag and add them to their own bag.
- Ask the kids how it feels to have less candy than their friend.
- Ask the kids how it felt to have their candy taken from them.
- Explain that even though people are sometimes mean to us, Jesus still wants us to show them love.
- Tell the child who played the tax collector to return the candy they took.

Acting the Part
Supplies Needed: Costumes (optional).
- Have the kids act out the story as you read it.

Read these verses out of a children's Bible while the kids do their hands-on activity. After reading the verses, engage the kids by asking questions about the text. Below are some questions to get you started.

Lesson Time Verses
Luke 19:1-4
Luke 19:5-7
Luke 19:8-10

Discussion Questions
1. Have you ever climbed a tree? Is it hard?
2. How far do you think Zacchaeus had to run to be able to climb a tree to see Jesus?
3. Do you think he was tired by the time he got into the tree?
4. How do you think Jesus knew Zacchaeus' name?
5. Why do you think Jesus wanted to stay at his house?
6. Zacchaeus used to steal money from people because he was a dishonest tax collector. After meeting Jesus he decided to stop stealing. Why do you think that is?
7. Did Jesus come to save just the good people, or did He come to save the not so good people too?

DISCOVERING PRAYER

Snack time can be a great time to teach preschoolers about prayer. You can also take prayer requests, review previous prayer requests, and receive praise reports.

1. Thinking about Zacchaeus, are there any kids you can think of that might not be so fun to be around that you can be a friend to?
2. If you see someone who doesn't have any friends, what kinds of things can you pray for that person?
3. What if we're the person who doesn't have a friend to play with? What can we pray then?

LET'S CREATE!

Hand print craft
Supplies Needed: Brown construction paper, scissors, glue, crayons, cotton balls, ink pad.
- Trace each child's hand and part of their arm on brown construction paper.
- Help the kids cut the hands out.
- Help the kids glue the hand cutouts onto another piece of paper.
- Give the kids ink pads and let them use their fingerprints to put leaves on their tree.
- Let the kids glue cotton balls above the tree for clouds.
- Let the kids color other decorations on their pictures.
- Encourage the kids to draw Zacchaeus in the tree.

Snack Craft
Supplies Needed: Pretzel sticks, pretzel rods, marshmallows, green food coloring or food sprinkles.
- Before class, cut up several marshmallows into small pieces and put food coloring on them or dip them in the sprinkles for the leaves.
- Place bowls of food stuff on the table.
- Let the kids create a tree out of the food.

LESSON 4: JESUS HELPS HIS FRIENDS

Supplies Needed for this Lesson:

Fish Crackers	Pretzels	3 Baskets	Spoons
Towel	Bread	Costumes	Paint
Paper	Paint Smocks	Paint Brushes	Crayons

LET'S PLAY A GAME!

Individual Play

My Friend May I?
Supplies Needed: None.
- Have all the kids stand in a line facing you.
- Let the kids take turns saying "My friend, May I…" (take 3 baby steps, 1 giant leap, etc.)
- The first one to reach you gets to take your place.
- Play until all the kids get to be at the front.

Multiple Play

Fish & Loaves Relay
Supplies Needed: Fish crackers, pretzels, 3 baskets, and spoons.
- Divide the kids into two teams.
- Place one basket on a table where both teams will be able to reach it.
- Give each team a basket and a spoon.
- Have one child from each team run to the basket, scoop up the fish and loaves with their spoon and take it back to their basket.
- The kids must then hand the spoon to the next child.
- When the central basket is empty the game ends.
- The team with the most food in their basket wins.
- Dropped food doesn't count.

MEMORY VERSE

Read the memory verse to the kids, showing them the hand motions to help them learn it. Have the kids repeat the verse with you a couple times while doing the hand motions.

I Am - Point up.
With you - Point to someone.
Always - Point up with one finger and move it in a circular motion.

> Copy and cut out the memory verse cards for this month so the kids can take them home to practice!

LET'S LEARN GOD'S WORD!

> ## Teacher Preparation
> Before class, choose one of the following Hands-On Activities for the kids to do while you read the story.

Multiplying Basket
Supplies Needed: Two baskets, towel, and bread.
- Before class starts, break the bread into small pieces and cover it with the towel.
- Take two of the pieces and place them in the other basket.
- Show the kids the basket with the two pieces in it.
- Have the covered basket nearby, don't let the kids peek in it.
- Explain that you've brought a treat to share with them.
- When they point out there isn't enough for everyone, tell them they're right.
- Tell the kids that Jesus had a similar problem once. He had only a small basket of fish and bread and more than 5,000 people to feed.
- Ask the kids how you feed so many people with so little food.
- Tell the kids that Jesus performed a miracle.
- As you're talking, grab a couple pieces of bread from the covered basket and hide them in your hands.
- Take one of the small pieces of bread in the uncovered bowl and break it in half. Drop the pieces you're hiding into the basket with the pieces you just broke.
- Continue doing this as you tell the story of Jesus and the loaves of fish.
- When the lesson is done, show the kids the basket and let them eat the bread.

Acting the part
Supplies Needed: Costumes (optional).
- Let the kids act out the story as you tell it.

Read these verses out of a children's Bible while the kids do their hands-on activity. After reading the verses, engage the kids by asking questions about the text. On the next page are some questions to get you started.

Lesson Time Verses
John 6:1-7
John 6:8-11
John 6:12-14

LET'S LEARN GOD'S WORD!

Discussion Questions

1. Have you ever had to share food or candy with someone?
2. Did you like sharing or did you want to keep it all for yourself?
3. Jesus fed over 5,000 people with two loaves of bread and five small fish. Do you think you could share that meal with 5,000 people?
4. Why did Jesus create food for people?
5. Wouldn't it be so cool to see a miracle like that happen?
6. Jesus wants to make sure everyone is taken care of, do you think Jesus wants us to make sure the people around us are taken care of?
7. What if it's people we don't know very well, like a new kid in class?

DISCOVERING PRAYER

Snack time can be a great time to teach preschoolers about prayer. You can also take prayer requests, review previous prayer requests, and receive praise reports.

1. Are there things your family needs that we can pray and ask God to give you?
2. Why do you think it's important to pray for things we need?
3. If God says all we have to do is pray for things we need, does that mean we can pray for new toys and we'll get them?
4. What are some things we need?

LET'S CREATE!

Paint a Picture
Supplies Needed: Paper, paint, paint smocks, brushes.
- Have the kids paint a picture of today's lesson.

Draw a Picture
Supplies Needed: Paper, crayons.
- Have the kids draw a picture of something they learned today.

LESSON 5: GOD'S FRIEND ABRAHAM

Supplies Needed for this Lesson:

Costumes	Play-Doh	Cookie Cutters	String Licorice
Marshmallows	Stick Pretzels	Toothpicks	Paper
Animals Crackers	Paint Smocks	Paint Brushes	Paint

LET'S PLAY A GAME!

Individual Play

Father Abraham
Supplies Needed: None.
- This game will get the wiggles out of the kids.
- Sing the song "Father Abraham".
- Each time through have the kids start moving another part of their body.

>Father Abraham, had many sons.
>Many sons had Father Abraham.
>I am one of them. And so are you.
>So let's all praise the Lord, Right Arm.
>(Left Arm, Right Leg, Left Leg, Head, Spin Around.)

Multiple Play

Red Light, Green Light
Supplies Needed: None.
- Have the kids line up on one side of the room facing you.
- Tell the kids that sometimes it's hard to wait for things we want, but waiting is also a good thing.
- When you say "Green Light" the kids can start walking toward you.
- When you say "Red Light" the kids must stop.
- If anyone keeps going on "Red Light", they must start over at the beginning.

MEMORY VERSE

Read the memory verse to the kids, showing them the hand motions to help them learn it. Have the kids repeat the verse with you a couple times while doing the hand motions.

I Am - Point up.
With you - Point to someone.
Always - Point up with one finger and move it in a circular motion.

> Copy and cut out the memory verse cards for this month so the kids can take them home to practice!

LET'S LEARN GOD'S WORD!

> **Teacher Preparation**
> Before class, choose one of the following Hands-On Activities for the kids to do while you read the story.

Acting the Part
Supplies Needed: Costumes (optional).
- Have the kids act out the story while you read it.

A Play-Doh Scene
Supplies Needed: Play-Doh, cookie cutters.
- Have the kids create the characters from the story out of Play-Doh as you tell the story.

Read these verses out of a children's Bible while the kids do their hands-on activity. After reading the verses, engage the kids by asking questions about the text. Below are some questions to get you started.

> **Lesson Time Verses**
> Genesis 18:1-7
> Genesis 18:8-15
> Genesis 21:1-5
> Genesis 22:1-6
> Genesis 22:7-13

Discussion Questions

1. What did God promise to Abraham?
2. Why did God ask Abraham to sacrifice his son?
3. Do you think you could give something up for God, a favorite toy or blanket maybe?
4. Why do you think God sometimes wants us to give things up?
5. Do you think it's because He has something even better for us?
6. How old do you think your parents were when you were born?
7. Did you know Abraham was 100 years old when Isaac was born?
8. Do you know anyone who is 100 years old?
9. Why do you think God called Abraham His friend?
10. Do you want to be friends with God?
11. How do we become friends with God?

DISCOVERING PRAYER

Snack time can be a great time to teach preschoolers about prayer. You can also take prayer requests, review previous prayer requests, and receive praise reports.

1. Have you ever had to wait for something for a long time? If so, what?
2. When we have to wait a long time for something, what can we pray to help us wait?
3. Do you think it would be hard to pray for patience when you really want something? Why?

LET'S CREATE!

Snack Craft
Supplies Needed: String licorice, stick pretzels, marshmallows, toothpicks, and animal crackers.
- Have each child build an altar with marshmallows and toothpicks.
- Help the kids tie a bundle of pretzels together with a piece of licorice for the sticks on top.
- Give each child an animal cracker to us as an offering on top of their altar.

Paint a Picture
Supplies Needed: Paper, paint, paint smocks, brushes.
- Give each child a piece of paper.
- Have them paint a picture about today's lesson.

AUGUST MEMORY VERSE CARDS

Matthew 28:20
"I am with you always."

Matthew 28:20
"I am with you always."

Matthew 28:20
"I am with you always."

Matthew 28:20
"I am with you always."

Matthew 28:20
"I am with you always."

Matthew 28:20
"I am with you always."

Matthew 28:20
"I am with you always."

Matthew 28:20
"I am with you always."

SEPTEMBER
GOD IS OUR HEALER

OVERVIEW

God didn't just die on the cross for our sins. He took all sickness and disease as well. These lessons will show Jesus as our Healer and what that means for us.

Memory Verse

Acts 9:34
"Jesus Christ heals you"

Hand Motions

Jesus Christ
Point up.

Heals
Place one hand, palm up in front of you. Make a fist, thumb up, with the other hand and place it on your open palm.

You
Point to someone.

LESSON 1: Jesus Heals a Paralyzed Man
When Jesus walked the earth, people did some crazy things just to be healed by Him. This lesson explores how four friends helped a man by tearing open a roof and lowering him down into the presence of Jesus.

LESSON 2: Jesus gives His Friends Power to Heal
This lesson explores the scripture where Jesus gives power to His disciples to heal the sick. The kids will discover that they too have this power inside them.

LESSON 3: Jesus Heals a Blind Man
Jesus used some unusual methods to heal people at times. This lesson will explore the blind man that Jesus healed by making mud and putting it on the man's eyes.

LESSON 4: Jesus Heals a Man's Daughter
Having a family member that's sick can be a stressful time. This lesson will explore the story of Jairus asking Jesus to help his daughter.

LESSON 5: Jesus Raises Lazarus
This lesson will explore Jesus' friendship with Lazarus, Mary and Martha and the raising of Lazarus back to life.

LESSON 1: JESUS HEALS A PARALYZED MAN

Supplies Needed for this Lesson:

Opaque Bag	Strips of Cloth	Costumes	Envelopes
Q-Tips	Band-Aids	Gauze Pads	Popsicle Sticks
Crayons	Construction Paper	Glue	
Small Objects from Around the Room			

LET'S PLAY A GAME!

Individual Play

Naming Objects
Supplies Needed: Small items from around the room, opaque bag.
- Before class, collect several items from around the classroom and place them in an opaque bag.
- Tell the kids when your eyes don't work you have to use your other senses to identify items. Such as touching, smelling, tasting and hearing.
- Have the kids reach into the bag one at a time and grasp an item.
- See if they can figure out what the item is just by touching it.
- At the end, pull all the items out so they can see if they were correct.

Multiple Play

Healing Tag
Supplies Needed: Strips of cloth.
- Pick one child to be sickness and one child to be healing.
- Give all the other children a strip of cloth and have them tie it on one of their legs.
- Tell the kids the leg with the cloth is broken. They will have to hop on the other leg.
- When the game starts, healing will try to tag all the kids hopping around on one foot.
- When healing tags someone, they can use both legs to run from sickness.
- Sickness will try to tag any child who has been healed.
- If sickness tags a child who has been healed, they have to go back to hopping on one leg until they are tagged by healing again.
- If everyone is running around healed the game is over.
- Rotate kids to be healing and sickness.

MEMORY VERSE

Read the memory verse to the kids, showing them the hand motions to help them learn it. Have the kids repeat the verse with you a couple times while doing the hand motions.

Jesus Christ - Point up.
Heals - Place one hand, palm up in front of you. Make a fist, thumb up, with the other hand and place it on your open palm.
You - Point to someone.

> Copy and cut out the memory verse cards for this month so the kids can take them home to practice!

LET'S LEARN GOD'S WORD!

> ### Teacher Preparation
> Before class, choose one of the following Hands-On Activities for the kids to do while you read the story.

No Legs
Supplies Needed: Long strips of cloth.
- Have all the kids sit on the floor. Tie their legs together at their ankles, knees and tops of their legs. Have the kids try to get up and walk around.
- Give the kids an everyday task to do like pick up toys.
- Ask the kids how it would feel if they could never use their legs again.
- Explain that Jesus helped a man who couldn't use his legs, be able to walk again.

Acting the Part
Supplies Needed: Costumes (optional).
- Have the kids act out the story as you read it.

Read these verses out of a children's Bible while the kids do their hands-on activity. After reading the verses, engage the kids by asking questions about the text. On the next page are some questions to get you started.

> **Lesson Time Verses**
> Mark 2:1-4
> Mark 2:5-10
> Mark 2:11-12

LET'S LEARN GOD'S WORD!

Discussion Questions

1. Have you ever seen someone healed?
2. Have you ever been sick with a cold? You got better after a while right?
3. Did anyone pray for you while you were sick?
4. God created our bodies to heal themselves. Sometimes they aren't able to do that and we need to receive healing directly from God. Do you think, if God has given us the power to heal, He wants us to be sick?
5. Do you think the paralyzed man was thankful to be able to walk again?

DISCOVERING PRAYER

Snack time can be a great time to teach preschoolers about prayer. You can also take prayer requests, review previous prayer requests, and receive praise reports.

1. Does anyone feel sick, or have scratches or owies?
2. God has given us the power to heal people just by using faith and our words. Would anyone like to pray for those who aren't feeling well or who have an owie?

LET'S CREATE!

Doctors Bag
Supplies Needed: Envelopes, Band-Aids, Q-tips, Popsicle sticks, gauze pads, and crayons.
- Give each child an envelope.
- Let the kids decorate the outside of the envelope.
- Let the kids put Band-Aids, Q-tips, Popsicle sticks and gauze pads in their envelope.

Mats
Supplies Needed: Strips of colored construction paper, glue.
- Have the kids place several strips of colored paper in a row.
- Show the kids how to weave other strips of paper through the rows of paper.
- When the kids have finished their mats, help them glue the ends in place to keep it together.

LESSON 2: JESUS GIVES HIS FRIENDS POWER TO HEAL

Supplies Needed for this Lesson:

Ball	Towels	Balloons	Strips of Cloth
Costumes	Paper	Scissors	Band-Aids
Marker	Crayons	Glue	Construction Paper

LET'S PLAY A GAME!

Individual Play

Knees Relay
Supplies Needed: Ball.
- Have the kids form a line. Give the first child in line a ball.
- Have the kids walk a short distance and back with the ball between their knees.
- The kids can't touch the ball unless it falls out, then they can only place it back between their knees.

Multiple Play

Man on a Mat Race
Supplies Needed: Towels, balloons.
- Divide the kids into groups of no more than four.
- Give each team a towel and a balloon.
- Tell the kids the balloon is the man on the mat and they are trying to get him to Jesus.
- Have each child on each team grab a corner of the towel.
- Place the balloon on each towel.
- Have the kids race from one end of the room to the other.
- If the balloon falls off, they must start again at the beginning.
- The first team to finish wins.

MEMORY VERSE

Read the memory verse to the kids, showing them the hand motions to help them learn it. Have the kids repeat the verse with you a couple times while doing the hand motions.

Jesus Christ - Point up.
Heals - Place one hand, palm up in front of you. Make a fist, thumb up, with the other hand and place it on your open palm.
You - Point to someone.

> Copy and cut out the memory verse cards for this month so the kids can take them home to practice!

LET'S LEARN GOD'S WORD!

Teacher Preparation
Before class, choose one of the following Hands-On Activities for the kids to do while you read the story.

No Arms
Supplies Needed: Long strips of cloth.
- Have all the kids stand in a line.
- Tie their arms to their sides.
- Have the kids try to do simple tasks like putting a toy away, or writing their name.
- Explain that some people have arms that don't work and they have to find new ways of doing things.
- Tell the kids that God wants everyone healed, even people who are missing arms or legs.

Acting the Part
Supplies Needed: Costumes (optional).
- Have the kids act out the story as you read it.

Read these verses out of a children's Bible while the kids do their hands-on activity. After reading the verses, engage the kids by asking questions about the text. Below are some questions to get you started.

Lesson Time Verses
Matthew 10:1

Discussion Questions

1. Who makes us feel better when we're sick?
2. Are doctors the only ones that can make us feel better?
3. Are you all followers of God?
4. What is a follower of God?
5. What do followers of God do?
6. Did you know that besides reading the Bible and praying, followers of God also pray for people to be healed?
7. Is anyone feeling sick today?
8. Would you guys like to practice praying for healing for each other?

DISCOVERING PRAYER

Snack time can be a great time to teach preschoolers about prayer. You can also take prayer requests, review previous prayer requests, and receive praise reports.

1. Do you think there is any kind of sickness God can't heal?
2. When we find out someone is sick, what can we do?

LET'S CREATE!

Jesus Heals Hearts
Supplies Needed: Paper hearts, marker, Band-Aids, scissors, crayons.
- Before class, cut out several large paper hearts and write "Jesus Heals Sick Hearts" on them.
- Give each child a heart.
- Let the kids decorate their hearts with crayons and Band-Aids.

Jesus Heals
Supplies Needed: Construction paper, scissors, marker, crayons, Band-Aids, and glue.
- Before class, take several pieces of construction paper and write "One Touch From Jesus Heals" at the top of them.
- Give each child one of the papers.
- Trace each child's hand and help them cut the hands out.
- Let the kids glue the hand cutouts to the written on paper.
- Give each child two Band-Aids. Have the kids make a cross with the Band-Aids and place the cross on the copy of their hand.

LESSON 3: JESUS HEALS A BLIND MAN

Supplies Needed for this Lesson:

Opaque Bag	Strips of Cloth	Masking Tape	Costumes
Paper	Crayons	Paint	Paint Brushes
Paint Smocks	Small Objects From Around the Room		

LET'S PLAY A GAME!

Individual Play

Naming Objects
Supplies Needed: Small items from around the room, opaque bag.
- Before class, collect several items from around the classroom and place them in an opaque bag.
- Tell the kids when your eyes don't work, you have to use your other senses to identify items. Such as touching, smelling, tasting and hearing.
- Have the kids reach into the bag one at a time and grasp an item.
- See if they can identify what the item is just by touching it.
- At the end, pull all the items out so they can see if they were correct.

Multiple Play

Obstacle Course
Supplies Needed: Strips of cloth, random items from around the room, masking tape.
- Before class, create an obstacle course and use masking tape to show the way through the course.
- Divide the kids up into teams of two.
- Have one child in each team blindfolded.
- The other child must guide the blindfolded child through the course.
- At the end of the course, the kids switch places and the child who was blindfolded guides the other child back to the start.

MEMORY VERSE

Read the memory verse to the kids, showing them the hand motions to help them learn it. Have the kids repeat the verse with you a couple times while doing the hand motions.

Jesus Christ - Point up.
Heals - Place one hand, palm up in front of you. Make a fist, thumb up, with the other hand and place it on your open palm.
You - Point to someone.

> Copy and cut out the memory verse cards for this month so the kids can take them home to practice!

LET'S LEARN GOD'S WORD!

Teacher Preparation
Before class, choose one of the following Hands-On Activities for the kids to do while you read the story.

No Eyes
Supplies Needed: Strips of cloth.
- Have all the kids stand in a line.
- Tie a cloth around their eyes so they can't see.
- Have the kids try to do simple tasks like putting a toy away, or finding an object.
- Explain that some people have eyes that don't work and they have to find a new way of doing things.
- Tell the kids that God wants everyone healed, even people who have eyes that don't work.

Acting the Part
Supplies Needed: Costumes (optional).
- Have the kids act out the story while you read it.

Read these verses out of a children's Bible while the kids do their hands-on activity. After reading the verses, engage the kids by asking questions about the text. Below are some questions to get you started.

Lesson Time Verses
John 9:1-6
John 9:7-11

Discussion Questions

1. How do you think it would feel if you couldn't use your eyes to see things? Would it be hard?
2. What kinds of things would you miss seeing if you didn't have any eyes?
3. How do you think the blind man in our story felt when he saw for the first time?
4. Do you think it would be cool to pray for someone who was blind and they suddenly started to see again?
5. What do you think about Jesus making mud out of his spit?
6. Would you want spit on your face?
7. What if it was the only way you could get healed?

DISCOVERING PRAYER

Snack time can be a great time to teach preschoolers about prayer. You can also take prayer requests, review previous prayer requests, and receive praise reports.

1. When can we pray for other people?
2. What kind of future does God want us to have?
3. Do you think God wants people to be blind or to be missing arms or legs?

LET'S CREATE!

Paint a Picture
Supplies Needed: Paper, paint, paint smocks, brushes.
- Have the kids paint a picture about the lesson.

Draw a Picture
Supplies Needed: Paper, crayons.
- Have the kids draw a picture of something they learned today.

LESSON 4: JESUS HEALS A MAN'S DAUGHTER

Supplies Needed for this Lesson:

Strips of Cloth	Ball	Costumes	Paper	Crayons
Scissors	Band-Aids	Marker		

LET'S PLAY A GAME!

Knees Relay
Supplies Needed: Ball.
- Have the kids form a line.
- Give the first child in line a ball.
- Have the kids walk a short distance and back with the ball between their knees.
- The kids can't touch the ball unless it falls out, then they can only place it back between their knees.

Healing Tag
Supplies Needed: Strips of cloth.
- Pick one child to be sickness and one child to be healing.
- Give all the other children a strip of cloth and have them tie it on one of their legs.
- Tell the kids that whatever leg the strip of cloth is on, is broken and they have to hop on the other leg.
- When the game starts, healing will try to tag all the kids as they hop around on one foot.
- When healing tags someone they can use both legs to run from sickness.
- Sickness will try to tag any child who has been healed.
- If sickness tags a child who has been healed, they have to go back to hopping on one leg until they are tagged by healing again.
- If everyone is running around healed the game is over.
- Rotate kids to be healing and sickness.

MEMORY VERSE

Read the memory verse to the kids, showing them the hand motions to help them learn it. Have the kids repeat the verse with you a couple times while doing the hand motions.

Jesus Christ - Point up.
Heals - Place one hand, palm up in front of you. Make a fist, thumb up, with the other hand and place it on your open palm.
You - Point to someone.

> Copy and cut out the memory verse cards for this month so the kids can take them home to practice!

LET'S LEARN GOD'S WORD!

> **Teacher Preparation**
> Before class, choose one of the following Hands-On Activities for the kids to do while you read the story.

Acting the Part
Supplies Needed: Costumes (optional).
- Have the kids act out the story as you read it.

No Legs
Supplies Needed: Long strips of cloth.
- Have all the kids sit on the floor.
- Tie their legs together at their ankles, knees and tops of their legs.
- Have the kids try to get up and walk around.
- Give the kids an everyday task to do like pick up toys.
- Ask the kids how it would feel if they could never use their legs again.
- Explain that Jesus helped a man who couldn't use his legs be able to walk again.

Read these verses out of a children's Bible while the kids do their hands-on activity. After reading the verses, engage the kids by asking questions about the text. Below are some questions to get you started.

Lesson Time Verses
Mark 5:21-24
Mark 5:35-40
Mark 5:41-43

Discussion Questions

1. Do you think Jairus was really worried about his daughter?
2. Do you think your parents worry about you when you're sick?
3. How do you think the girl's parents felt when Jesus healed her?
4. How do you think your parents feel when you start feeling better after you've been sick?
5. Do you think Jesus likes it when we pray for people to be healed?
6. Why don't you all practice praying for each other.

DISCOVERING PRAYER

Snack time can be a great time to teach preschoolers about prayer. You can also take prayer requests, review previous prayer requests, and receive praise reports.

1. What are some things we can pray and thank Jesus for today?
2. If you see someone crying, what can you do to help them?
3. Do you always have to be quiet when you're praying?

LET'S CREATE!

Draw a Picture
Supplies Needed: Paper, crayons.
- Have the kids draw a picture about today's lesson.

Mended Hearts
Supplies Needed: Heart cut-outs, Band-Aids, marker, and scissors.
- Before class, cut out several hearts for the kids.
- Give each child a heart and a Band-Aid.
- Have the kids stick their Band-Aid on their heart.
- On each heart write "Jesus" on each Band-Aid write "Mends".

LESSON 5: JESUS RAISES LAZARUS

Supplies Needed for this Lesson:

Opaque Bag	2 Rolls of Toilet Paper	Costumes	Paper Plates
Strips of Cloth	Scissors	Hot Dogs	Googly Eyes
Paper Towels	Glue	Crescent Roll Dough	
Random Toys	Cardboard Toilet Paper Rolls		

LET'S PLAY A GAME!

Individual Play

Naming Objects

Supplies Needed: Small items from around the room, opaque bag.
- Before class, collect several items from around the classroom and place them in an opaque bag.
- Tell the kids that when your eyes don't work, you have to use your other senses to identify items. Such as touching, smelling, tasting and hearing.
- Have the kids reach into the bag one at a time and grasp an item.
- See if they can identify what the item is just by touching it.
- At the end, pull all the items out so they can see if they were correct.

Multiple Play

Lazarus Come Forth

Supplies Needed: Two rolls of toilet paper.
- Divide the kids into two teams.
- Give each team a roll of toilet paper.
- Have one person from each team stand in the middle of their team.
- Have the kids wrap their teammate in the toilet paper.
- When the kids are covered, have the team members shout "Lazarus, Come Forth!"
- The child can then break out of the toilet paper.
- Let each child be wrapped.

MEMORY VERSE

Read the memory verse to the kids, showing them the hand motions to help them learn it. Have the kids repeat the verse with you a couple times while doing the hand motions.

Jesus Christ - Point up.
Heals - Place one hand, palm up in front of you. Make a fist, thumb up, with the other hand and place it on your open palm.
You - Point to someone.

> Copy and cut out the memory verse cards for this month so the kids can take them home to practice!

LET'S LEARN GOD'S WORD!

Teacher Preparation
Before class, choose one of the following Hands-On Activities for the kids to do while you read the story.

Acting the Part
Supplies Needed: Costumes (optional).
- Have the kids act out the story as you read it.

No Arms
Supplies Needed: Long strips of cloth.
- Have all the kids stand in a line.
- Tie their arms to their sides.
- Have the kids try to do simple tasks like putting a toy away, or writing their name.
- Explain that some people have arms that don't work and they have to find new ways of doing things.
- Tell the kids God wants everyone healed, even people who are missing arms or legs.

Read these verses out of a children's Bible while the kids do their hands-on activity. After reading the verses, engage the kids by asking questions about the text. Below are some questions to get you started.

Lesson Time Verses
John 11:1-14   John 11:34-35
John 11:17-23   John 11:38-44
John 11:25-32

Discussion Questions

1. Do any of you know of someone who has died?
2. How would you feel if your best friend died?
3. Jesus' friend Lazarus died and He was very sad. Do you think it's strange that Jesus was sad when He was planning on raising Lazarus from the dead?
4. How do you think Lazarus' sisters felt when Lazarus walked out of the tomb?
5. We've been learning a lot about healing this month. Did you know that raising people from the dead was part of the power God gave to us when He gave us power to heal?
6. How does it make you feel knowing God has given you the power to heal people?

DISCOVERING PRAYER

Snack time can be a great time to teach preschoolers about prayer. You can also take prayer requests, review previous prayer requests, and receive praise reports.

1. Do you think it's important to learn how to hear God's voice?
2. Do you think prayer is all about talking to God, or is it about hearing from God too?
3. Does anyone want to pray for the class so we can all learn to hear God's voice better?

LET'S CREATE!

TP Roll Mummy
Supplies Needed: Toilet paper rolls, googly eyes, glue, paper towel, and scissors.
- Give each child a toilet paper roll, a paper towel and two googly eyes.
- Have the kids tear their paper towel into strips.
- Help the kids glue the strips of paper towel on the toilet paper roll.
- Help the kids glue the googly eyes on the toilet paper roll.

Lazarus Rolls
Supplies Needed: Crescent roll dough, hot dogs, and paper plates.
- Before class, cut the hot dogs in half and make small strips from the dough.
- Give each child a plate and two halves of a hotdog.
- Place bowls of dough on the table.
- Let the kids wrap their hotdogs with the dough.
- Tell the kids to have their parents cook their snack when they get home.
- Or, if you have the means, cook the snack for them.

SEPTEMBER MEMORY VERSE CARDS

| Acts 9:34 | Acts 9:34 |
| "Jesus Christ heals you." | "Jesus Christ heals you." |

Acts 9:34
"Jesus Christ heals you."

Acts 9:34
"Jesus Christ heals you."

Acts 9:34
"Jesus Christ heals you."

Acts 9:34
"Jesus Christ heals you."

Acts 9:34
"Jesus Christ heals you."

Acts 9:34
"Jesus Christ heals you."

Acts 9:34
"Jesus Christ heals you."

Acts 9:34
"Jesus Christ heals you."

OCTOBER
WE ARE GOD'S HELPERS

OVERVIEW

Jesus had people who helped Him when He was on the earth and He has many more helpers now. These lessons will show the kids they too can be helpers of God. **This includes service project ideas the kids can do.**

Memory Verse

Philippians 4:13
"I can do all things because God gives me strength."

Hand Motions

I
Point to self.

Can do all things
Hold one hand in a fist. Move it away from you and make an "L" shape with your pointer and thumb.

Because God
Point up.

Gives me
Point to self.

Strength
Show your muscles.

LESSON 1: Jesus' 12 Helpers
This lesson will go over the verses that show Jesus gathering His helpers. The kids will discover Jesus is still gathering helpers today and they can be one of them.

LESSON 2: Noah Helped God Save the World
Noah and the flood is a classic story for preschoolers. This lesson will explore the idea that because Noah obeyed God, he helped God save the human race and the world.

LESSON 3: Esther Helped God Save the Jews
Esther was a reluctant Queen, but even though she didn't ask for the position she was given, God was still able to use her to save the Jews.

LESSON 4: How We Can Be God's Helpers
This lesson will focus on different service projects the kids can do as helpers of God.

LESSON 5: Paul Helped Jesus Spread Good News
Paul had an amazing conversion and lived his life passionately for the Lord. This lesson will show the kids that even after Jesus went back to heaven, He was still calling out for helpers and He still is.

LESSON 1: JESUS' 12 HELPERS

Supplies Needed for this Lesson:

Beanbag	Chairs	Costumes	Play-Doh	Paint
Cookie Cutters	Paint Smocks	Paint Brushes	Scissors	Glue
Tissue Paper	Paper	Cotton Balls	Crayons	
Stickers	Music	Misc. Craft Supplies		

LET'S PLAY A GAME!

Individual Play

Beanbag Compliments
Supplies Needed: Beanbag.
- Have the kids form a circle.
- Throw the beanbag to a child and tell them something nice.
- Have the child throw the beanbag to someone else. Have them say something nice about that child. Continue until all the kids have received at least one compliment.
- Encourage the kids to say things like "you make me laugh" or "you are a good listener" etc.

Multiple Play

Cooperative Musical Chairs
Supplies Needed: Chairs, music.
- Place chairs in a line, back to back with one less chair than there are children.
- Turn the music on and have the kids walk around the chairs.
- When the music stops, the kids have to find a chair, but they must find a way for all the kids to have a seat. When they've accomplished this, take one chair away.
- Continue with game until the kids can no longer figure out how they can all have a seat. Encourage the kids to use kind words and help each other.

MEMORY VERSE

Read the memory verse to the kids, showing them the hand motions to help them learn it. Have the kids repeat the verse with you a couple times, doing the hand motions.

I - Point to self.
Can do all things - Hold one hand in a fist. Move it away from you and make an "L" shape with your pointer and thumb.
Because God - Point up.
Gives me - Point to self.
Strength - Show your muscles.

> Copy and cut out the memory verse cards for this month so the kids can take them home to practice!

LET'S LEARN GOD'S WORD!

Teacher Preparation
Before class, choose one of the following Hands-On Activities for the kids to do while you read the story.

Acting the Part
Supplies Needed: Costumes (optional).
- Have the kids act out the story while you read it.

A Play-Doh Scene
Supplies Needed: Play-Doh, cookie cutters.
- Have the kids create the characters from the story out of Play-Doh as you tell the story.

Read these verses out of a children's Bible while the kids do their hands-on activity. After reading the verses, engage the kids by asking questions about the text. Below are some questions to get you started.

Lesson Time Verses
Luke 5:1-5
Luke 5:6-11

Discussion Questions

1. Are you all good helpers at home?
2. What kinds of things do you help with?
3. Did you know God needs helpers too?
4. Why do you think God needs help?
5. Do you want to be one of God's helpers?
6. What do you think Jesus meant when He said His helpers would fish for people instead of fish?
7. Would you rather fish all day, or be one of God's helpers?

DISCOVERING PRAYER

Snack time can be a great time to teach preschoolers about prayer. You can also take prayer requests, review previous prayer requests, and receive praise reports.

1. Can we be God's helpers by remembering to pray?
2. Does God listen to us when we pray?
3. How do you know He listens?
4. Does God always say "Yes" when we pray for something?

LET'S CREATE!

Paint a Picture
Supplies Needed: Paper, paint, paint smocks, brushes.
- Have the kids paint a picture about today's lesson.

Create a Picture
Supplies Needed: Paper, tissue paper, scissors, glue, cotton balls, crayons, stickers, and miscellaneous craft supplies.
- Let the kids create a picture from craft supplies about today's lesson.

LESSON 2: NOAH HELPS GOD SAVE THE WORLD

Supplies Needed for this Lesson:

Water Table	Toy Boats, People & Animals	Costumes
Small Paper Plates	Cotton Balls	Yarn	Scissors
Glue	Toilet Paper Rolls	Cardstock	Hot Glue Gun
Rice or Beans	Stickers	Crayons	Egg Cartons
Paper	Random Toys		

LET'S PLAY A GAME!

Individual Play

Sink or Float
Supplies Needed: Water table or shallow plastic bin, random toys from around the room.
- Have the kids look at the items and try to guess which ones will sink or float.
- Let them test the toys. Let the kids get other toys from around the room.

Multiple Play

Memory Match
Supplies Needed: Memory cards from page 186 and 187.
- Mix up the cards and place them face-down on the table.
- Let each child turn over two cards.
- If the cards match, they can keep them.
- If the cards don't match, they turn them over again.
- Let the kids take turns until all the cards have been matched.

MEMORY VERSE

Read the memory verse to the kids, showing them the hand motions to help them learn it. Have the kids repeat the verse with you a couple times while doing the hand motions.

I - Point to self.
Can do all things - Hold one hand in a fist. Move it away from you and make an "L" shape with your pointer and thumb.
Because God - Point up.
Gives me - Point to self.
Strength - Show your muscles.

> Copy and cut out the memory verse cards for this month so the kids can take them home to practice!

MEMORY MATCH GAME

All Images © Angela E. Powell

1 Year of Sunday School Lessons for 3-5 year olds | Angela E. Powell

MEMORY MATCH GAME

All Images © Angela E. Powell

187

LET'S LEARN GOD'S WORD!

Teacher Preparation
Before class, choose one of the following Hands-On Activities for the kids to do while you read the story.

Water Play
Supplies Needed: Water table or shallow plastic bin, toy boats, toy people, and toy animals. Let the kids play out the story as you read it.

Acting the part
Supplies Needed: Costumes (optional).
Have the kids act out the story as you read it.

Read these verses out of a children's Bible while the kids do their hands-on activity. After reading the verses, engage the kids by asking questions about the text. Below are some questions to get you started.

Lesson Time Verses
Genesis 6:5-20
Genesis 6:22, 7:1-5
Genesis 7:17-24
Genesis 8:1-15
Genesis 9:11-16

Discussion Questions

1. Did you know Noah was one of God's helpers?
2. Before God asked Noah to build the Ark, it had never rained before. Do you think people laughed at Noah because he was building a big boat and telling people it was going to rain?
3. What do you think those people thought when all the animals started showing up?
4. What do you think those people thought when it finally started to rain?
5. Have you ever seen a rainbow? Aren't they pretty?
6. What is your favorite color in the rainbow?
7. Why did God send the rainbow?
8. Why did God flood the Earth?
9. Do you think it's hard for God to see bad things happening in the earth?
10. Do you think that is one reason He is looking for helpers, so we can help Him get rid of some of the bad things?

DISCOVERING PRAYER

Snack time can be a great time to teach preschoolers about prayer. You can also take prayer requests, review previous prayer requests, and receive praise reports.

1. When we pray, do we always have to ask God for things?
2. What are some things we can pray and thank God for today?

LET'S CREATE!

Rainbow Cloud
Supplies Needed: Small paper plates, cotton balls, colored yarn, scissors, and glue.
- Before class, cut rainbow colored yarn into similar lengths.
- Give each child a paper plate.
- On one side let the kids glue cotton balls on the plate.
- On the back side, let the kids glue pieces of yarn in a rainbow pattern.
- Take one piece of yarn and glue it to the top of the plate as a hanger.

Rain Stick
Supplies Needed: Toilet paper roll, egg carton, glue gun, rice or beans, stickers, crayons, glue and paper.
- Before class, trim egg carton cups so they fit into the ends of the toilet paper rolls.
- Give each child a toilet paper roll.
- Use the glue gun to glue one egg cup into one end of the roll.
- Let the kids pour some rice or beans inside.
- Glue the other egg cup to the other end.
- Help the kids glue strips of paper onto their rolls.
- Let the kids decorate with stickers and by coloring their rolls.

LESSON 3: ESTHER HELPS GOD SAVE THE JEWS

Supplies Needed for this Lesson:

Costumes	Props	Chairs	Music	Crown
Paper	Glitter	Stickers	Stapler	Glue
Crayons	Construction Paper			

LET'S PLAY A GAME!

Individual Play

Talent Show
Supplies Needed: Costumes (optional), props.
- Let the kids perform a talent show to show off their talents.

Multiple Play

Royal Musical Chairs
Supplies Needed: Chairs, music, crown.
- Line up two rows of chairs back to back, with one less chair than there are kids.
- Turn the music on.
- Have the kids walk around the chairs.
- When the music stops the kids must find a seat.
- The child who does not get a chair, gets to wear a crown the next round.
- Each round, have the child who is wearing the crown, hand the crown to the child who didn't find a seat.

MEMORY VERSE

Read the memory verse to the kids, showing them the hand motions to help them learn it. Have the kids repeat the verse with you a couple times while doing the hand motions.

I - Point to self.
Can do all things - Hold one hand in a fist. Move it away from you and make an "L" shape with your pointer and thumb.
Because God - Point up.
Gives me - Point to self.
Strength - Show your muscles.

> Copy and cut out the memory verse cards for this month so the kids can take them home to practice!

LET'S LEARN GOD'S WORD!

Teacher Preparation
Before class, choose one of the following Hands-On Activities for the kids to do while you read the story.

Acting the Part
Supplies Needed: Costumes (optional).
- Have the kids act out the story while you read it.

Talent Show
Supplies Needed: Costumes (optional), props.
- Let the kids perform a talent show to show off their talents.
- Between every couple of acts, read part of the story.

Read these verses out of a children's Bible while the kids do their hands-on activity. After reading the verses, engage the kids by asking questions about the text. Below are some questions to get you started.

Lesson Time Verses
Esther 1:10-12, 16, 19
Esther 2:1-4
Esther 2:8
Esther 2:10-17
Esther 3:5-6, 8-11
Esther 5:1-6
Esther 7:1-10

Discussion Questions

1. What would you do if you were a King or Queen?
2. How would you rule your kingdom?
3. Have you ever had to do something that seemed scary? What was it?
4. In our story Esther went to the King without being summoned by him.
5. Did you know that if the King had been in a bad mood that day, he could have killed Esther for coming to him?
6. Esther was a brave helper of God. What kinds of things can we do to help God?

DISCOVERING PRAYER

Snack time can be a great time to teach preschoolers about prayer. You can also take prayer requests, review previous prayer requests, and receive praise reports.

1. Did you know you can be a strong prayer warrior for God?
2. Why is it important to pray?
3. Why does God give us talents?
4. What talents do you have that you'd like God to use?
5. Who would like to pray and ask God to use our special talents in a special way?

LET'S CREATE!

Crowns
Supplies Needed: Construction paper, glitter, glue, stickers, and stapler.
- Before class, cut several pieces of construction paper in half length-wise in a zig-zag pattern.
- Give each child two pieces of construction paper.
- Let the kids decorate their crowns.
- Staple the two halves together and measure the child's head.
- Staple the end together and trim off the extra paper.

Draw a Picture
Supplies Needed: Paper, crayons.
- Let the kids draw pictures about today's lesson.

LESSON 4: HOW WE CAN BE GOD'S HELPERS

Supplies Needed for this Lesson:

Beanbag	Chairs	Jars	Ingredients for Cookies	Paper
Crayons	Markers	Pots	Dirt	Paint Smocks
Flowers	Water	Paint	Music	Paint Brushes

LET'S PLAY A GAME!

Individual Play

Beanbag Compliments
Supplies Needed: Beanbag.
- Have the kids form a circle.
- Throw the beanbag to a child and tell them something nice.
- Have the child throw the beanbag to someone else. Have them say something nice about that child. Continue until all the kids have received at least one compliment.
- Encourage the kids to say things like "you make me laugh" or "you are a good listener" etc.

Multiple Play

Cooperative Musical Chairs
Supplies Needed: Chairs, music.
- Place chairs in a line, back to back with one less chair than there are children.
- Turn the music on and have the kids walk around the chairs.
- When the music stops, the kids have to find a chair, but they must find a way for all the kids to have a seat. When they've accomplished this, take one chair away.
- Continue with game until the kids can no longer figure out how to all have a seat.
- Encourage the kids to use kind words and help each other.

MEMORY VERSE

Read the memory verse to the kids, showing them the hand motions to help them learn it. Have the kids repeat the verse with you a couple times, doing the hand motions.

I - Point to self.
Can do all things - Hold one hand in a fist. Move it away from you, make an "L" shape with your pointer and thumb.
Because God - Point up.
Gives me - Point to self.
Strength - Show your muscles.

> Copy and cut out the memory verse cards for this month so the kids can take them home to practice!

LET'S LEARN GOD'S WORD!

> ### Teacher Preparation
> Before class, choose one of the following Hands-On Activities for the kids to do while you read the story.

Cookie Mix for Smiles

Supplies Needed: Ingredients to make a cookie mix, jars.

- Have the kids put together cookie mix to give away at a nursing home, or women's shelter.
- If you can arrange it, take the kids on a field trip to deliver the cookie mix.
- You can also have the kids take the mix home and have the families make the deliveries.

Sponsor a Child

Supplies Needed: Paper, crayons, markers.

- Choose an organization that will allow you to sponsor a child. There is information about sponsoring children in the resource section of this book on page 240.
- Have the kids collect money for the sponsor.
- Have the kids create cards for the child they sponsor.

Planting for Seniors

Supplies Needed: Pots, dirt, flowers, water.

- Have the kids decorate flower pots.
- Help them plant flowers into the pots.
- Tell the kids the plants will be going to a senior center to cheer up some people who might be lonely.
- You can also send the pot home with a flyer explaining the service project and have the families deliver the flowers themselves. There are flyers you can copy in the resource section of this book on pages 236 and 237.
- If you are able to, you can also schedule a time for the kids to meet at a specific senior center and have them hand the plants out.

Discussion Questions

1. Do you think we're being God's helpers today?
2. What other ways can we be God's helpers?
3. Why do you think it's important for God to have helpers?
4. Do you think people will like the things we've made for them?

DISCOVERING PRAYER

Snack time can be a great time to teach preschoolers about prayer. You can also take prayer requests, review previous prayer requests, and receive praise reports.

1. What is another name for talking to God?
2. When can we pray?
3. What kinds of prayers are there?
4. What would a sad or scared prayer be?

LET'S CREATE!

Draw a Picture
Supplies Needed: Paper, crayons.
- Give each child a paper.
- Have them draw a picture of ways they can help others.

Paint a Picture
Supplies Needed: Paint, paint smocks, brushes, paper.
- Let the kids paint pictures of ways they can help others.

LESSON 5: PAUL HELPED JESUS SPREAD THE GOOD NEWS

Supplies Needed for this Lesson:

Costumes, Props, Chairs, Music, Crown, Paper, Crayons, Pencils, Markers, Paint, Glue, Scissors, Paint Smocks, Paint Brushes, Misc. Craft Supplies

LET'S PLAY A GAME!

Individual Play
Talent Show
Supplies Needed: Costumes (optional), props.
- Let the kids perform a talent show to show off their talents.

Multiple Play
Royal Musical Chairs
Supplies Needed: Chairs, music, crown.
- Line up two rows of chairs back to back, with one less chair than there are kids.
- Turn the music on.
- Have the kids walk around the chairs.
- When the music stops the kids must find a seat.
- The child who does not find a chair, gets to wear a crown the next round.
- Each round, have the child who is wearing the crown, hand the crown to the child who didn't find a seat.

MEMORY VERSE

Read the memory verse to the kids, showing them the hand motions to help them learn it. Have the kids repeat the verse with you a couple times, doing the hand motions.

I - Point to self.
Can do all things - Hold one hand in a fist. Move it away from you and make an "L" shape with your pointer and thumb.
Because God - Point up.
Gives me - Point to self.
Strength - Show your muscles.

> Copy and cut out the memory verse cards for this month so the kids can take them home to practice!

LET'S LEARN GOD'S WORD!

Teacher Preparation
Before class, choose one of the following Hands-On Activities for the kids to do while you read the story.

Acting the Part
Supplies Needed: Costumes (optional).
- Have the kids act out the story as you read it.

Draw a Picture
Supplies Needed: Paper, crayons, pencils and/or markers.
- Give each child a piece of paper.
- Ask them to draw a picture of something they learned from the lesson.

Read these verses out of a children's Bible while the kids do their hands-on activity. After reading the verses, engage the kids by asking questions about the text. Below are some questions to get you started.

Lesson Time Verses
Acts 9:1-9
Acts 9:10-19

Discussion Questions

1. Why do you think God changed Saul's name to Paul?
2. How do you think Saul felt when God blinded him and spoke to him the way He did?
3. Did you know it doesn't matter what you do in life, God can always find a way to use you?

DISCOVERING PRAYER

Snack time can be a great time to teach preschoolers about prayer. You can also take prayer requests, review previous prayer requests, and receive praise reports.

1. If you see someone who doesn't have any friends, what can you pray for that person?
2. What if we're the person who doesn't have friends? What can we pray then?

LET'S CREATE!

Paint a Picture
Supplies Needed: Paper, paint, paint smocks, brushes.
- Let the kids paint a picture from today's lesson.

Create a Picture
Supplies Needed: Miscellaneous craft supplies, paper, glue, and scissors.
- Let the kids create a picture from today's lesson with miscellaneous craft supplies.

OCTOBER MEMORY VERSE CARDS

Philippians 4:13
"I can do all things because God gives me strength."

Philippians 4:13
"I can do all things because God gives me strength."

Philippians 4:13
"I can do all things because God gives me strength."

Philippians 4:13
"I can do all things because God gives me strength."

Philippians 4:13
"I can do all things because God gives me strength."

Philippians 4:13
"I can do all things because God gives me strength."

Philippians 4:13
"I can do all things because God gives me strength."

Philippians 4:13
"I can do all things because God gives me strength."

NOVEMBER
GOD WANTS US TO BE THANKFUL

OVERVIEW

November is when we celebrate Thanksgiving. These lessons will show the importance of being thankful in every situation life throws at us. **The children will have an opportunity to participate in a service project this month.**

Memory Verse

Psalm 150:6
"Let everything that has breath praise the Lord."

Hand Motions

Let everything
Wave a hand in front of you, palm up.

That has breath
Point to your mouth.

Praise
Raise arms in the air and shake your hands.

The Lord
Point up.

LESSON 1: The 10 Lepers
10 lepers wanted to be healed and God granted their request. When only one came back, God asked a very important question. The kids will explore why it's important to give thanks.

LESSON 2: A Thankful Heart is Willing to Give
This lesson focuses on the temple that Solomon, David's son built. The kids will learn what it means to be willing to give.

LESSON 3: Jehoshaphat Defeats an Army
Jehoshaphat wanted to follow God, so when a large army showed up, Jehoshaphat went straight to God to find out what to do. This lesson will show that being thankful is a very powerful tool God has given us.

LESSON 4: Being Thankful No Matter What
This lesson will be a review of the month and give the kids an opportunity to be involved in a service project.

LESSON 5: Let Everything that has Breath Praise the Lord
This lesson will focus on our memory verse for the month. The kids will have a Thanksgiving party with special treats and dance music. The kids will celebrate the things God has done for us!

LESSON 1: THE 10 LEPERS

Supplies Needed for this Lesson:
Ball   2 Buckets   Costumes   Paper   Crayons
Markers   Glue   Scissors   Paint   Paint Smocks
Paint Brushes   20 Random Toys   Construction Paper

LET'S PLAY A GAME!

Individual Play
Thankful Hot Potato
Supplies Needed: Ball.
- Have the kids sit in a circle.
- Hand one child a ball.
- Tell the kids when the music starts to pass the ball around until the music stops.
- Whoever is holding the ball when the music stops has to say something they're thankful for.

Multiple Play
Giving Relay
Supplies Needed: Twenty small objects from around the room, two buckets.
- Tell the kids they will be learning how much God likes it when we give back to Him.
- Explain that God only asks us to give a small part of what we have to Him.
- Divide the kids into two teams.
- Have the objects piled on the table or floor where both teams will be able to get to them.
- Place the buckets next to the objects.
- Have the teams form lines.
- The first child will run to the pile, pick up an object and take it back to their team.
- The child will hand the object to the next person in line, who will hand it to the next child under his legs.
- The next child will hand it to the next child over their head and so on.
- The last child in line, will run to the bucket and put their item in.
- The first team to finish wins.
- Explain that out of all these items on the table, God only asks us to give a small part.
- You can play the game several times, letting different children be first and last in line.

MEMORY VERSE

Read the memory verse to the kids, showing them the hand motions to help them learn it. Have the kids repeat the verse with you a couple times while doing the hand motions.

Let everything - Wave a hand in front of you, palm up.
That has breath - Point to your mouth.
Praise - Raise arms in the air and shake your hands.
The Lord - Point up.

> Copy and cut out the memory verse cards for this month so the kids can take them home to practice!

LET'S LEARN GOD'S WORD!

> ### Teacher Preparation
> Before class, choose one of the following Hands-On Activities for the kids to do while you read the story.

Acting the Part
Supplies Needed: Costumes (optional).
- Have the kids act out the story as you read it.

Draw a Picture
Supplies Needed: Paper, crayons, pencils and/or markers.
- Give each child a piece of paper.
- Ask them to draw a picture of things they hear in the lesson today.

Read these verses out of a children's Bible while the kids do their hands-on activity. After reading the verses, engage the kids by asking questions about the text. Below are some questions to get you started.

> **Lesson Time Verses**
> Luke 17:11-14
> Luke 17:15-19

Discussion Questions

1. Have you ever gotten a present? Did you say thank you for the gift?
2. Have you ever given a present and the person didn't say thank you?
3. How did it make you feel?
4. How do you think Jesus felt when only one came back to give thanks?
5. What kinds of things are you thankful for?
6. When we're at home, how can we thank our parents?

DISCOVERING PRAYER

Snack time can be a great time to teach preschoolers about prayer. You can also take prayer requests, review previous prayer requests, and receive praise reports.

1. Do we always have to ask for things when we pray?
2. Why is it important to say thank you?
3. What are some things we can thank God for today?

LET'S CREATE!

Paint a Picture
Supplies Needed: Paper, paint, brushes, paint smocks.
- Give each child a piece of paper.
- Let the kids paint a picture about today's lesson.

Handprint Thankful Tree
Supplies Needed: Colored construction paper, scissors, and glue.
- Trace each child's hand and cut out several copies.
- While this is being done, give each child a piece of blank paper and have them draw a tree trunk.
- Have the kids glue their handprints onto their tree.
- Have the kids come up with things they are thankful for.
- Write what they say on the handprints.

LESSON 2: A THANKFUL HEART IS WILLING TO GIVE

Supplies Needed for this Lesson:

2 Buckets	Costumes	Paper	Paint	Paint Smocks
Paint Brushes	Envelopes	Crayons	Stickers	Scissors
Markers	Paper Plates	String	Hole Punch	Yellow Paper
Stapler	20 Random Toys			

LET'S PLAY A GAME!

Individual Play

Simon Says
Supplies Needed: None.
- Play a game of Simon Says with the kids.
- Instead of telling them to jump or skip or hop, say things like "Simon says name something you're thankful for." "Simon says, find a toy you're thankful for", etc.

Multiple Play

Giving Relay
Supplies Needed: Twenty small objects from around the room, two buckets.
- Tell the kids they will be learning how much God likes it when we give back to Him.
- Explain that God only asks us to give a small part of what we have to Him.
- Divide the kids into two teams.
- Have the objects piled on the table or floor where both teams will be able to get to them.
- Place the buckets next to the objects.
- Have the teams form lines.
- The first child will run to the pile, pick up an object and take it back to their team.
- The child will hand the object to the next person in line, who will hand it to the next child under his legs.
- The next child will hand it to the next child over their head and so on.
- The last child in line, will run to the bucket and put their item in.
- The first team to finish wins.
- Explain that out of all these items on the table, God only asks us to give a small part.
- You can play the game several times, letting different children be first and last in line.

MEMORY VERSE

Read the memory verse to the kids, showing them the hand motions to help them learn it. Have the kids repeat the verse with you a couple times while doing the hand motions.

Let everything - Wave a hand in front of you, palm up.
That has breath - Point to your mouth.
Praise - Raise arms in the air and shake your hands.
The Lord - Point up.

> Copy and cut out the memory verse cards for this month so the kids can take them home to practice!

LET'S LEARN GOD'S WORD!

Teacher Preparation
Before class, choose one of the following Hands-On Activities for the kids to do while you read the story.

Acting the Part
Supplies Needed: Costumes (optional).
- Have the kids act out the story as you read it.

Paint a Picture
Supplies Needed: Paper, paint, paint smocks, paint brushes.
- Give each child a piece of paper.
- Ask them to paint a picture of things they hear in the lesson today.

Read these verses out of a children's Bible while the kids do their hands-on activity. After reading the verses, engage the kids by asking questions about the text. Below are some questions to get you started.

> **Lesson Time Verses**
> 1 Chronicles 29:1-4
> 1 Chronicles 29:6-9
> 1 Chronicles 29:13-15

Discussion Questions

How do you think God feels when we give to others?
God spoke to David and told him Solomon, his son, was going to build the temple.
What did David do after God told him this?
When a lot of people get together and give, it makes everyone feel really happy. Do you think if you were the only one in the crowd who gave, you would still feel good?
What if you were the only one who didn't give?
How do you think you'd feel then?
What toys have you gotten recently? Are you thankful for the toys you have?

DISCOVERING PRAYER

Snack time can be a great time to teach preschoolers about prayer. You can also take prayer requests, review previous prayer requests, and receive praise reports.

1. Would anyone like to pray and thank God for giving us so much that we're able to give to others?
2. There are kids who don't have any toys to play with. What can we pray for them?

LET'S CREATE!

Tithing Envelope
Supplies Needed: Envelopes, crayons, stickers, marker.
- Before class, take several envelopes and write "Tithe" on the front.
- Give each child an envelope and let them decorate it.
- Tell the kids if they want to give to God, they can put it in the envelope to help them remember to bring it to church.

Gold Coins
Supplies Needed: Paper plates, stapler, string, hole punch, crayons, stickers, coin template from page 207, yellow paper, and scissors.
- Before class, make copies of the coins on yellow paper and cut several paper plates in half.
- Help the kids cut out a page of coins.
- Give each child two halves of a paper plate.
- Let the kids decorate the back of each plate with crayons and stickers.
- Help the kids staple their plates together to make a pouch.
- Use the hole punch to make holes in each side of the pouch.
- Give each child a piece of string and help them tie it to their pouch.
- Let the kids put their coins inside.

COINS CRAFT

$2 $2

$2 $2

$2 $2

LESSON 3: JEHOSHAPHAT DEFEATS AN ARMY

Supplies Needed for this Lesson:

Ball	Costumes	Paper	Crayons	Markers
Duct Tape	Plastic Eggs	Stapler	Beans or Rice	Stickers
Paper Bowls				

LET'S PLAY A GAME!

Individual Play
Simon Says
Supplies Needed: None.
- Play a game of "Simon Says" with the kids.
- Instead of telling them to jump or skip or hop, say things like "Simon says, name something you're thankful for." "Simon says, find a toy you're thankful for" etc.

Multiple Play
Thankful Hot Potato
Supplies Needed: Ball.
- Have the kids sit in a circle.
- Hand one child a ball.
- Tell the kids when the music starts to pass the ball around until the music stops.
- Whoever is holding the ball when the music stops has to say something they're thankful for.

MEMORY VERSE

Read the memory verse to the kids, showing them the hand motions to help them learn it. Have the kids repeat the verse with you a couple times while doing the hand motions.

Let everything - Wave a hand in front of you, palm up.
That has breath - Point to your mouth.
Praise - Raise arms in the air and shake your hands.
The Lord - Point up.

> Copy and cut out the memory verse cards for this month so the kids can take them home to practice!

LET'S LEARN GOD'S WORD!

Teacher Preparation
Before class, choose one of the following Hands-On Activities for the kids to do while you read the story.

Acting the Part
Supplies Needed: Costumes (optional).
- Have the kids act out the story as you read it.

Draw a Picture
Supplies Needed: Paper, crayons, pencils and/or markers.
- Give each child a piece of paper.
- Ask them to draw a picture of things they hear in the lesson today.

Read these verses out of a children's Bible while the kids do their hands-on activity. After reading the verses, engage the kids by asking questions about the text. Below are some questions to get you started.

Lesson Time Verses
2 Chronicles 20:2-4
2 Chronicles 20:5-6, 12-13, 15-18
2 Chronicles 20:20-25

Discussion Questions

1. Have you ever wanted to do a really good job for your mom and dad?
2. What were you trying to do?
3. Jehoshaphat wanted to do exactly what God wanted him to do. Do you think it can be hard to do what God wants us to do? Why?
4. Do you ever wonder what God wants you to do?
5. How do we find out what He wants us to do?
6. How did Jehoshaphat discover what God wanted him to do?
7. How do you think the army felt when they realized the praise and worship team was winning the battle?
8. Why do you think the people praising God were so powerful?
9. Do you think when we praise God it has that same power? Why?

DISCOVERING PRAYER

Snack time can be a great time to teach preschoolers about prayer. You can also take prayer requests, review previous prayer requests, and receive praise reports.

1. What are some things we don't want to do that we can ask God to help us with?
2. Do you think if you ask God to help you with something He will?
3. If we know God is going to help us, do you think we should say thank you?

LET'S CREATE!

Praise Maracas
Supplies Needed: Plastic eggs, beans or rice, duct tape.
- Give each child two plastic spoons and a plastic egg.
- Let the kids fill half their egg with beans.
- Have the kids put their egg together.
- Hold the egg between the spoons so they are hugging the egg.
- Let the kids choose a color of duct tape.
- Help the kids wrap the duct tape around the spoons and egg.

Praise Drums
Supplies Needed: Paper bowls, stapler, crayons, stickers.
- Give each child two paper bowls.
- Have the kids place one bowl upside down on top of the other bowl.
- Help the kids staple the edges.
- Let the kids decorate their drums.

LESSON 4: BEING THANKFUL NO MATTER WHAT

Supplies Needed for this Lesson:

2 Buckets	Shoe Boxes	Paper	Crayons
Gallon Bags	Finger Paint	Markers	Brads
Scissors	Paint	Paint Brushes	Paint Smocks
Big & Small Paper Plates		20 Random Toys	

LET'S PLAY A GAME!

Individual Play
Simon Says
Supplies Needed: None.
- Play a game of "Simon Says" with the kids.
- Instead of telling them to jump or skip or hop, say things like "Simon says, name something you're thankful for." "Simon says, find a toy you're thankful for" etc.

Multiple Play
Giving Relay
Supplies Needed: Twenty small objects from around the room, two buckets.
- Tell the kids they will be learning how much God likes it when we give back to Him.
- Explain that God only asks us to give a small part of what we have to Him.
- Divide the kids into two teams.
- Have the objects piled on the table or floor where both teams will be able to get to them.
- Place the buckets next to the objects.
- Have the teams form lines.
- The first child will run to the pile, pick up an object and take it back to their team.
- The child will hand the object to the next person in line, who will hand it to the next child under his legs.
- The next child will hand it to the next child over their head and so on.
- The last child in line, will run to the bucket and put their item in.
- The first team to finish wins.
- Explain that out of all these items on the table, God only asks us to give a small part.
- You can play the game several times, letting different children be first and last in line.

MEMORY VERSE

Read the memory verse to the kids, showing them the hand motions to help them learn it. Have the kids repeat the verse with you a couple times while doing the hand motions.

Let everything - Wave a hand in front of you, palm up.
That has breath - Point to your mouth.
Praise - Raise arms in the air and shake your hands.
The Lord - Point up.

> Copy and cut out the memory verse cards for this month so the kids can take them home to practice!

LET'S LEARN GOD'S WORD!

> ### Teacher Preparation
> Before class, choose one of the following Hands-On Activities for the kids to do while you read the story.

Act it Out
Supplies Needed: None.
- Read the scenarios to the kids. Have them act them out if you wish.
- Have the kids say how they can be thankful in each situation.

1. Your mom brings a bag of candy home. She says you can have one piece but you were hoping for three. How can you be thankful?
2. You get to church and find a new girl playing with your favorite toy. You are sad. How can you be thankful?
3. Your dad tells you he is going to take you to the zoo on Saturday, but it's raining on Saturday and you can't go. How can you be thankful?
4. You and your best friend want to have a sleepover. You ask your parents, but they say no. How can you be thankful?
5. You get a card in the mail for your birthday from your Grandma. You hope there is money inside, but there isn't. How can you be thankful?
6. You're at church and find your best friend isn't there. How can you be thankful?
7. You ask your parents if you can have some ice cream. They tell you there is no ice cream and they aren't going to go get any. How can you be thankful?
8. Your parents tell you they are going to be going through all of your toys and getting rid of the old ones. How can you be thankful?
9. The older kids at church are doing a play and you want to be in it too, but your teacher says you are too young to be part of it this year. How can you be thankful?
10. You're at the swimming pool and your parents tell you it's time to go. You don't want to leave. How can you be thankful?

LET'S LEARN GOD'S WORD!

> **Teacher Preparation**
> Before class, choose one of the following Hands-On Activities for the kids to do while you read the story.

Operation Christmas Child
Supplies Needed: Donated items, shoe boxes.
- If your church takes part in this organization, have the kids help put boxes together.
- If your church doesn't take part in this, have the preschoolers collect items for boxes.
- More information can be found in the resource section of this book on page 240.

Compassion International
Supplies Needed: Money donations, paper, and crayons.
- Have the kids make cards for a sponsored child.
- Or collect money for the Unsponsored Children's Fund.
- More information can be found in the resource section of this book on page 240.

Homeless Kits
Supplies Needed: Donated items, gallon bags.
- Have the kids put together bags for the homeless.
- If you can arrange a field trip, have the kids deliver the bags to a homeless shelter.
- Or let each child take some of the bags home and let the families deliver the bags.
- More information can be found in the resource section of this book on page 241

Discussion Questions

1. Do you think the people who will receive these items will be thankful?
2. A lot of the people we're sending items to don't have very much. What do you think it would be like if you didn't have any shoes to wear?
3. What do you think it would be like if you didn't have soap to wash your hair with?
4. What do you think it would be like if you didn't have a home, but had to live outside in the cold?
5. Thinking about the people who will be receiving these items, how can we be thankful?

DISCOVERING PRAYER

Snack time can be a great time to teach preschoolers about prayer. You can also take prayer requests, review previous prayer requests, and receive praise reports.

1. What are some things we can talk about with God when we pray?
2. How can we pray when we've done something wrong?
3. When we pray, do we always have to ask God for things?
4. What are some things we can pray and thank God for today?

LET'S CREATE!

Handprint Turkey
Supplies Needed: Finger paint, paper, markers.
- Let the kids choose what colors of paint they want to put on their fingers and hands.
- Help the kids make a hand print on a piece of paper.
- Let the kids decorate the thumb to look like a turkey head.
- Help the kids write things they are thankful for around the handprint.

Thankful Wheel
Supplies Needed: Big paper plates, small paper plates, brads, paint, brushes, paint smocks, markers, scissors and crayons.
- Give each child one small and one big paper plate.
- Let the kids paint the edge of the big plate and the whole little plate.
- When the plates are dry, draw an 8-piece "pie" in the center of the big plate.
- Let the kids color the middle of their plate.
- With a marker have each child come up with 8 things they're thankful for.
- Help the kids write them in the spaces on the pie.
- On the small plate, cut out a slice about the size of one piece of the pie.
- Connect the two plates together with a brad.
- Show the kids how they can move the small plate around to reveal the things they're thankful for.

LESSON 5: LET EVERYTHING THAT HAS BREATH PRAISE THE LORD

Supplies Needed for this Lesson:
Ball	Praise Music	Musical Instruments	Special Snack
Tape	Large Rubber Bands	Shoe Boxes w/ Lids	String
Bells	Scissors		

LET'S PLAY A GAME!

Individual Play
Simon Says
Supplies Needed: None.
- Play a game of Simon Says with the kids.
- Instead of telling them to jump or skip or hop, say things like "Simon says, name something you're thankful for." "Simon says, find a toy you're thankful for." etc.

Multiple Play
Thankful Hot Potato
Supplies Needed: Ball.
- Have the kids sit in a circle.
- Hand one child a ball.
- Tell the kids when the music starts they have to pass the ball around until the music stops.
- Whoever is holding the ball when the music stops has to say something they're thankful for.

MEMORY VERSE

Read the memory verse to the kids, showing them the hand motions to help them learn it. Have the kids repeat the verse with you a couple times while doing the hand motions.

Let everything - Wave a hand in front of you, palm up.
That has breath - Point to your mouth.
Praise - Raise arms in the air and shake your hands.
The Lord - Point up.

> Copy and cut out the memory verse cards for this month so the kids can take them home to practice!

LET'S LEARN GOD'S WORD!

Teacher Preparation
Before class, choose one of the following Hands-On Activities for the kids to do while you read the story.

Praise Party!
Supplies Needed: Praise music, musical instruments (can be handmade), special snack. (doughnuts, cookies, ice cream etc.)
- Turn some music on. Tell the kids we're going to have a party today to thank Jesus for all He's done for us.
- Encourage the kids to praise God and dance for God.
- Remind them of the memory verse.

Discussion Questions

1. Why is it important to be thankful?
2. What are some things you're thankful for?
3. How can we show people we're thankful?
4. How can we show God we're thankful?

DISCOVERING PRAYER

Snack time can be a great time to teach preschoolers about prayer. You can also take prayer requests, review previous prayer requests, and receive praise reports.

1. Who wants to pray and thank God for all the things He's blessed us with?
2. Who can name five things they're thankful for?

LET'S CREATE!

Shoebox Guitars
Supplies Needed: Shoe boxes with lids, large rubber bands, tape, and scissors.
- Give each child a shoe box and let them tape the lid down.
- Cut out a hole in the middle of the lid.
- Let the kids string rubber bands over the box and let them play their guitar.

Praise Bells
Supplies Needed: String, bells.
- Let the kids put bells on their string.
- Help them tie it off.

NOVEMBER MEMORY VERSE CARDS

Psalm 150:6
"Let everything that has breath praise the Lord."

Psalm 150:6
"Let everything that has breath praise the Lord."

Psalm 150:6
"Let everything that has breath praise the Lord."

Psalm 150:6
"Let everything that has breath praise the Lord."

Psalm 150:6
"Let everything that has breath praise the Lord."

Psalm 150:6
"Let everything that has breath praise the Lord."

Psalm 150:6
"Let everything that has breath praise the Lord."

Psalm 150:6
"Let everything that has breath praise the Lord."

DECEMBER
JESUS IS THE GREATEST GIFT

OVERVIEW

Christmas is when we celebrate the birth of our Savior. The lessons in December will break down the Christmas story into small chunks. The kids will take a closer look at why that time in history was so important.

Memory Verse

James 1:17
"Every good and perfect gift is from above"

Hand Motions

Every good
Place your fingers on your mouth. Take your hand a few inches from your mouth.

And perfect
Make an OK sign with your fingers.

Gift
Hold out your hands palms up, crossed over each other.

Is from above
Point up.

LESSON 1: God Talks to Mary & Joseph
This lesson focuses on the angel coming to visit Mary and Joseph. The kids will get a glimpse into why Joseph was uncomfortable at discovering Mary's pregnancy and the rules in place at the time.

LESSON 2: Mary & Joseph Make a Long Journey
Mary and Joseph had to travel a long distance for the census. In this lesson the kids will find out what a census is and why it was necessary. They will also discover how uncomfortable Mary must have been on that journey.

LESSON 3: Jesus is Born
The birth of Jesus, although humble, is an incredible story. The angels singing and shepherds showing up to see Jesus. The kids will discover how amazing this night was and God's role in bringing everything together.

LESSON 4: Wise Men Bring Gifts to Jesus
The wise men looked to the sky to see God's messages there. They discovered a strange star that led them right to Jesus. The kids will learn a little bit about who the wise men were and why they decided to follow a star.

LESSON 5: Jesus is the Best Present to Give Others
Jesus is the reason for the season and He's the best gift anyone could receive. This lesson will review the month and the kids will discover how to share Jesus with others.

LESSON 1: GOD TALKS TO MARY & JOSEPH

Supplies Needed for this Lesson:

Nativity Toy Set	Chairs	Music	Costumes
Play-Doh	Cookie Cutters	Glue	Scissors
Marker	Paper	Crayons	
Misc. Craft Supplies	Brown & Green Construction Paper		

LET'S PLAY A GAME!

Individual Play
Nativity Hide & Seek
Supplies Needed: Nativity toy set.
- Before class, hide all the toys from the Nativity Set around the room.
- Have the kids try to find all the pieces and put them together on the table.

Multiple Play
Musical Chairs
Supplies Needed: Chairs, music.
- Set up two rows of chairs back to back.
- Have one fewer chairs than there are kids.
- Tell the kids each chair is an Inn, whoever doesn't get to a chair when the music stops has to go stay in the stable with baby Jesus.

MEMORY VERSE

Read the memory verse to the kids, showing them the hand motions to help them learn it. Have the kids repeat the verse with you a couple times while doing the hand motions.

Every good - Place your fingers on your mouth. Take your hand a few inches from your mouth.
And perfect - Make an OK sign with your fingers.
Gift - Hold out your hands palms up, crossed over each other.
Is from above - Point up.

> Copy and cut out the memory verse cards for this month so the kids can take them home to practice!

LET'S LEARN GOD'S WORD!

Teacher Preparation
Before class, choose one of the following Hands-On Activities for the kids to do while you read the story.

Acting the Part
Supplies Needed: Costumes (optional).
- Have the kids act out the story while you read it.

A Play-Doh Scene
Supplies Needed: Play-Doh, cookie cutters.
- Have the kids create the characters from the story out of Play-Doh as you tell the story.

Read these verses out of a children's Bible while the kids do their hands-on activity. After reading the verses, engage the kids by asking questions about the text. Below are some questions to get you started.

Lesson Time Verses
Luke 1:26-32
Luke 1:34-38
Matthew 1:19-24

Discussion Questions

1. What is Christmas all about?
2. Who can tell me the whole story of Christmas?
3. We only read part of the Christmas story today, what was your favorite part?
4. In the time when Jesus was born, it was considered a sin worthy of death to have a baby when you weren't married. Why do you think Joseph almost changed his mind about marrying Mary after he found out she was going to have a baby?
5. Do you think Mary was scared when she found out she was going to have a baby?
6. Mary wasn't sure why she'd been chosen to be Jesus' mother, but she trusted God. Do you think God can ask us to do something that might be hard for us?

DISCOVERING PRAYER

Snack time can be a great time to teach preschoolers about prayer. You can also take prayer requests, review previous prayer requests, and receive praise reports.

1. In our lesson today, God sent an angel to speak to Mary and Joseph. Can you think of a time when God spoke to you?
2. Mary was a young girl when she had Jesus. She probably had some fear about it. Are there any fears you have that you'd like us to pray for?

LET'S CREATE!

Hand Tree
Supplies Needed: Brown and green construction paper, glue, scissors, marker, miscellaneous craft supplies.
- On green construction paper, trace each child's hand a few times.
- Help the kids cut out the drawings of their hands.
- Give each child a wide strip of brown paper.
- Help them glue it to another piece of paper.
- Let the kids glue their hand cutouts upside down on the paper in the form of a Christmas tree.
- Let the kids decorate their trees with miscellaneous craft supplies.

Draw a Picture
Supplies Needed: Paper, crayons.
- Have the kids draw a picture of the Christmas story.

LESSON 2: MARY & JOSEPH MAKE A LONG JOURNEY

Supplies Needed for this Lesson:

Nativity Toy Set	Butcher Paper	Tape	Paint Brushes
Paint Smocks	Paint	Costumes	Glue
Popsicle Sticks	Buttons	Stickers	String
Misc. Craft Supplies	No-Bake Clay	String	Dowel Rod

LET'S PLAY A GAME!

Individual Play

Nativity Hide & Seek
Supplies Needed: Nativity toy set.
- Before class, hide all the toys from the Nativity Set around the room.
- Have the kids try to find all the pieces and put them together on the table.

Multiple Play

Christmas Mural
Supplies Needed: Butcher paper, tape, brushes, paint smocks, paint.
- Before class, tape a long strip of butcher paper to the table or wall.
- Have the kids work together to make a Christmas scene.

MEMORY VERSE

Read the memory verse to the kids, showing them the hand motions to help them learn it. Have the kids repeat the verse with you a couple times while doing the hand motions.

Every good - Place your fingers on your mouth. Take your hand a few inches from your mouth.
And perfect - Make an OK sign with your fingers.
Gift - Hold out your hands palms up, crossed over each other.
Is from above - Point up.

> Copy and cut out the memory verse cards for this month so the kids can take them home to practice!

LET'S LEARN GOD'S WORD!

> **Teacher Preparation**
> Before class, choose one of the following Hands-On Activities for the kids to do while you read the story.

Acting the Part
Supplies Needed: Costumes (optional).
- Have the kids act out the story while you read it.

Follow Mary & Joseph
Supplies Needed: None.
- Have the kids play Follow the Leader with you.
- Have them encounter things Mary and Joseph might have encountered on their trip.

Read these verses out of a children's Bible while the kids do their hands-on activity. After reading the verses, engage the kids by asking questions about the text. Below are some questions to get you started.

Lesson Time Verses
Luke 2:1-5

Discussion Questions

1. Do you remember what we talked about last week?
2. Do you remember what the angel told Mary and Joseph?
3. Have you ever made a long trip in a car or on a plane? Did you like it? Did you get tired or bored?
4. Mary and Joseph didn't have cars when they were alive. They only had horses, camels and donkeys. Which animal did Mary ride on?
5. Do you think it would be comfortable riding a donkey for very long? It was probably even less comfortable because she was about to have a baby.
6. Can you imagine having a baby moving inside you and having to sit on a donkey all day for many days?
7. A census is when the government counts how many people there are in certain places. Why do you think that's important to know?

DISCOVERING PRAYER

Snack time can be a great time to teach preschoolers about prayer. You can also take prayer requests, review previous prayer requests, and receive praise reports.

1. Have you ever taken a trip in a car or a plane?
2. Did you or your parents pray for a safe trip?
3. Why do you think it's important to pray for a safe trip?

LET'S CREATE!

Christmas Tree Ornament
Supplies Needed: Popsicle sticks, paint, glue, buttons, stickers or other small decorations, and string.
- Have the kids glue a triangle together out of the Popsicle sticks.
- Let the kids paint their sticks.
- When the paint is dry, have the kids decorate their trees.
- Tie a string to the triangle so the kids can hang it on their tree at home.

Handprint Ornaments
Supplies Needed: No-bake clay, paint, dowel, string or ribbon.
- Give each child a small ball of clay.
- Have the kids press the ball into a flat shape.
- Help the kids press their hands into the dough.
- Use the dowel rod to put a hole through the dough.
- Put string or ribbon through the hole and tie it off.
- Let the dough dry for a while.
- Let the kids paint their ornaments or, if there isn't enough time, have the kids decorate their ornaments at home.

LESSON 3: JESUS IS BORN

Supplies Needed for this Lesson:

Nativity Toy Set
Paper
Popsicle Sticks
Misc. Craft Supplies
Chairs
Glitter
Crayons
Music
Glue
Scissors
Costumes
Tissue Paper

LET'S PLAY A GAME!

Individual Play
Nativity Hide & Seek
Supplies Needed: Nativity toy set.
- Before class, hide all the toys from the Nativity Set around the room.
- Have the kids try to find all the pieces and put them together on the table.

Multiple Play
Musical Chairs
Supplies Needed: Chairs, music.
- Set up two rows of chairs back to back.
- Have one fewer chairs than there are kids.
- Tell the kids each chair is an Inn, whoever doesn't get to a chair when the music stops has to go stay in the stable with baby Jesus.

MEMORY VERSE

Read the memory verse to the kids, showing them the hand motions to help them learn it. Have the kids repeat the verse with you a couple times while doing the hand motions.

Every good - Place your fingers on your mouth. Take your hand a few inches from your mouth.
And perfect - Make an OK sign with your fingers.
Gift - Hold out your hands palms up, crossed over each other.
Is from above - Point up.

> Copy and cut out the memory verse cards for this month so the kids can take them home to practice!

LET'S LEARN GOD'S WORD!

Teacher Preparation
Before class, choose one of the following Hands-On Activities for the kids to do while you read the story.

Acting the Part
Supplies Needed: Costumes (optional).
- Have the kids act out the story while you read it.

Nativity Play Set
Supplies Needed: Nativity play set.
- Let the kids tell the story of Jesus' birth with the nativity set.

Read these verses out of a children's Bible while the kids do their hands-on activity. After reading the verses, engage the kids by asking questions about the text. Below are some questions to get you started.

Lesson Time Verses
Luke 2:6-14
Luke 2:15-20

Discussion Questions

1. Do you remember what we talked about last week?
2. Why did Mary and Joseph have to make a long journey?
3. Do you remember what a census is?
4. Do you think the shepherds were happy to hear about Jesus?
5. How did the Shepherds know about God sending a Savior?
6. In the Old Testament God was always telling the Hebrew people He was going to send them a Savior. When the angels showed up and told the Shepherds Jesus had arrived, do you think they remembered all the stories from long before?
7. Why do we celebrate the birth of Jesus?
8. What did Jesus do when He grew up?

DISCOVERING PRAYER

Snack time can be a great time to teach preschoolers about prayer. You can also take prayer requests, review previous prayer requests, and receive praise reports.

1. What do you think it was like sleeping in a stable with the animals?
2. Why is it important that Jesus was born?
3. Would anyone like to pray and thank Jesus for coming to save us?

LET'S CREATE!

Create a Picture
Supplies Needed: Paper, glitter, glue, tissue paper, Popsicle sticks, and miscellaneous craft supplies.
- Let the kids create a Christmas picture using miscellaneous craft supplies.

Christmas Cards
Supplies Needed Paper, miscellaneous craft supplies, crayons, glue, and scissors.
- Give each child a piece of paper.
- Help them fold it in half.
- Let the kids create a Christmas card for their family.

LESSON 4: WISE MEN BRING GIFTS TO JESUS

Supplies Needed for this Lesson:

Nativity Toy Set	Butcher Paper	Tape	Paint Brushes
Paint Smocks	Paint	Costumes	Glue
Construction Paper	String	Paper Plates	Scissors
Tissue Paper			

LET'S PLAY A GAME!

Individual Play
Nativity Hide & Seek
Supplies Needed: Nativity toy set.
- Before class, hide all the toys from the Nativity Set around the room.
- Have the kids try to find all the pieces and put them together on the table.

Multiple Play
Christmas Mural
Supplies Needed: Butcher paper, tape, brushes, paint smocks, paint.
- Before class, tape a long strip of butcher paper to the table or wall.
- Have the kids paint their favorite things about Christmas.

MEMORY VERSE

Read the memory verse to the kids, showing them the hand motions to help them learn it. Have the kids repeat the verse with you a couple times while doing the hand motions.

Every good - Place your fingers on your mouth. Take your hand a few inches from your mouth.
And perfect - Make an OK sign with your fingers.
Gift - Hold out your hands palms up, crossed over each other.
Is from above - Point up.

> Copy and cut out the memory verse cards for this month so the kids can take them home to practice!

LET'S LEARN GOD'S WORD!

Teacher Preparation
Before class, choose one of the following Hands-On Activities for the kids to do while you read the story.

Acting the Part
Supplies Needed: Costumes (optional).
- Have the kids act out the story while you read it.

Nativity Play Set
Supplies Needed: Nativity play set.
- Let the kids tell the story of Jesus' birth with the nativity set.

Read these verses out of a children's Bible while the kids do their hands-on activity. After reading the verses, engage the kids by asking questions about the text. Below are some questions to get you started.

Lesson Time Verses
Matthew 2:1-8
Matthew 2:9-12

Discussion Questions

1. Do you remember what we talked about last week?
2. What happened when Jesus was born?
3. How did the wise men know which star to follow?
4. Have you ever looked at the stars?
5. Have you ever seen any pictures in the stars?
6. The wise men studied the stars and God created the stars so they went in patterns. Do you think there is anything in the Bible about what the wise men might have seen in the sky?

DISCOVERING PRAYER

Snack time can be a great time to teach preschoolers about prayer. You can also take prayer requests, review previous prayer requests, and receive praise reports.

1. Why did the wise men follow the star?
2. How do you follow a star?
3. The wise men brought gifts to Jesus. Do you think praying can be a gift to Jesus?

LET'S CREATE!

Paper Chain Christmas Tree
Supplies Needed: Construction paper, glue, string.
- Before class, cut strips of green construction paper.
- Let the kids create six circles with the paper.
- Glue the circles together in a pyramid.
- Tie a piece of string to the top circle.

Christmas Wreath
Supplies Needed: Paper plates, tissue paper, glue, scissors, string.
- Before class, cut out the middle of several paper plates.
- Give each child the ring of the plate.
- Let them glue pieces of tissue paper on the wreath.
- Tie string around the wreath so the kids can hang it.

LESSON 5: JESUS IS THE BEST PRESENT TO GIVE OTHERS

Supplies Needed for this Lesson:
Nativity Toy Set   Chairs   Music   Costumes
Cotton Balls   Popsicle Sticks   Glitter   Glue
Scissors   Paper   Misc. Craft Supplies

LET'S PLAY A GAME!

Individual Play
Nativity Hide & Seek
Supplies Needed: Nativity toy set.
- Before class, hide all the toys from the Nativity Set around the room.
- Have the kids try to find all the pieces and put them together on the table.

Multiple Play
Musical Chairs
Supplies Needed: Chairs, music.
- Set up two rows of chairs back to back.
- Have one fewer chairs than there are kids.
- Tell the kids each chair is an Inn, whoever doesn't get to a chair when the music stops has to go stay in the stable with baby Jesus.

MEMORY VERSE

Read the memory verse to the kids, showing them the hand motions to help them learn it. Have the kids repeat the verse with you a couple times while doing the hand motions.

Every good - Place your fingers on your mouth. Take your hand a few inches from your mouth.
And perfect - Make an OK sign with your fingers.
Gift - Hold out your hands palms up, crossed over each other.
Is from above - Point up.

> Copy and cut out the memory verse cards for this month so the kids can take them home to practice!

LET'S LEARN GOD'S WORD!

Teacher Preparation
Before class, choose one of the following Hands-On Activities for the kids to do while you read the story.

Acting the Part
Supplies Needed: Costumes (optional).
- Have the kids act out the story while you read it.

Nativity Play Set
Supplies Needed: Nativity play set.
- Let the kids tell the story of Jesus' birth with the nativity set.

Discussion Questions
1. Who can tell me the whole story of Christmas and Jesus' birth?
2. What did the angel tell Mary and Joseph?
3. Why did Mary and Joseph have to take a long journey?
4. What happened when Jesus was born?
5. Why did the angels go to the Shepherds?

DISCOVERING PRAYER

Snack time can be a great time to teach preschoolers about prayer. You can also take prayer requests, review previous prayer requests, and receive praise reports.

1. What can we thank Jesus for now that Christmas is over?
2. When can we pray for other people?

LET'S CREATE!

Snowflake Ornament
Supplies Needed: Popsicle sticks, cotton balls, glitter, and glue.
- Give each child three Popsicle sticks.
- Help the kids glue their sticks together in the middle to create a snowflake.
- Let the kids glue cotton balls onto the sticks.
- Let the kids sprinkle glitter on their project.

Create a Picture
Supplies Needed: Miscellaneous craft supplies, paper, glue, and scissors.
- Let the kids create a Christmas picture from miscellaneous craft supplies.

DECEMBER MEMORY VERSE CARDS

James 1:17
"Every good and perfect gift is from above"

James 1:17
"Every good and perfect gift is from above"

James 1:17
"Every good and perfect gift is from above"

James 1:17
"Every good and perfect gift is from above"

James 1:17
"Every good and perfect gift is from above"

James 1:17
"Every good and perfect gift is from above"

James 1:17
"Every good and perfect gift is from above"

James 1:17
"Every good and perfect gift is from above"

REFERENCE GUIDE

In these pages, you will find helpful information and resources to make lessons and service projects even better. I have included flyers you can hand out to members of your church and the parents of the children in your class.

If you have questions or comments about this curriculum feel free to contact me at authoraepowell@gmail.com or drop me note on my website at www.angelaepowell.com.

Several lessons require you to have a jail cell. Below, are several ideas on how to create a jail cell for your classroom.

1. A large box. If the box is big enough you may be able to fit more than one child inside. You can also take the box apart and use it to create a jail cell in a corner of your room by creating a fence out of the box.

2. Paper chains. Make several paper chains and hang them from a doorway. If you have a stage in your classroom, you can hang the chains from there.

3. Rope. Take rope and attach it to two walls with eye hooks so the rope is taut. This option allows a lot more kids to be inside the jail cell as you can place the rope where you need it. This is best in a corner of your room.

4. Duct tape jail cell. This one takes some patience! Take long strips of duct tape and fold them over. When you have four or five separate strips, take another long strip of duct tape and put it on the floor sticky side up. Line your finished strips on top of the new strip about six inches apart. Fold the new strip of tape over. Make another strip about six inches from the one you just created. Make sure to sandwich the strips in between.

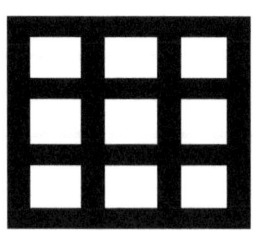

Throw & Tell Balls

You can find Throw & Tell balls on Amazon.com, or through Group Publishing. You can also create your own. There are several examples of how to do this on the internet or on Pinterest.

Copy this handout and have it placed inside the bulletins at your church. These are all items that can be recycled and repurposed in your classroom for games, lessons and crafts. If you have people in your church who know how to sew, you can ask for fabric donations and ask people to volunteer to make costumes for the kids to wear.

Donations Needed

The youngest members of our church like to have fun! We learn about the Bible by playing games, getting hands-on with Bible stories, and making great crafts. Some of the things we make require a few items that most people have in their homes. Would you be willing to recycle some things for our classroom? Here is the list of things we need.

Small Boxes	Strips of Cloth	Gently Used Kids Dress-Up Clothes
Medium Boxes	Paper Towel Rolls	Plastic Soda Bottles
Large Boxes	Toilet Paper Rolls	Plastic Lids, All Sizes
Shoe Boxes	Egg Cartons	Empty Jars w/Lids
Yarn		

Thank You!

Donations Needed

The youngest members of our church like to have fun! We learn about the Bible by playing games, getting hands-on with Bible, stories and making great crafts. Some of the things we make require a few items that most people have in their homes. Would you be willing to recycle some things for our classroom? Here is the list of things we need.

Small Boxes	Strips of Cloth	Gently Used Kids Dress-Up Clothes
Medium Boxes	Paper Towel Rolls	Plastic Soda Bottles
Large Boxes	Toilet Paper Rolls	Plastic Lids, All Sizes
Shoe Boxes	Egg Cartons	Empty Jars w/Lids
Yarn		

Thank You!

This is another handout you can place in the bulletin. This is for the service project "Planting for Seniors". If you want to participate in this service project, pick a senior center and give them a call. Set up a day and time when you can bring the pots in.

Donations Needed for Service Project

This month our preschoolers will be learning about serving others. They will be putting together small flower pots that will be delivered to _____ Senior Center. If you would like to get involved with what our kids are doing, please consider donating some of the following items.

Small Flower Pots   Potting Soil   Seeds or Flowers

Thank You!

Donations Needed for Service Project

This month our preschoolers will be learning about serving others. They will be putting together small flower pots that will be delivered to _____ Senior Center. If you would like to get involved with what our kids are doing, please consider donating some of the following items.

Small Flower Pots   Potting Soil   Seeds or Flowers

Thank You!

Donations Needed for Service Project

This month our preschoolers will be learning about serving others. They will be putting together small flower pots that will be delivered to _____ Senior Center. If you would like to get involved with what our kids are doing, please consider donating some of the following items.

Small Flower Pots   Potting Soil   Seeds or Flowers

Thank You!

Take home parent flyer for "Planting for Seniors" service project.

Service Project

Dear Parents,

This month your preschoolers will be learning about serving others. They will be putting together small flower pots to be delivered to _____. If you would like to get involved with what our kids are doing, please consider donating the following items.

Small Flower Pots   Potting Soil   Seeds or Flowers

We would like the children to be able to hand the flowers out themselves. We can do this in two ways. Each child can take a flower pot home that you can then deliver to the senior center. Or, if you are available on _____ we can meet at the senior center at _____ A.M/P.M.

Please let us know what you prefer by this date: _____.

Thank You!

Service Project

Dear Parents,

This month your preschoolers will be learning about serving others. They will be putting together small flower pots to be delivered to _____. If you would like to get involved with what our kids are doing, please consider donating the following items.

Small Flower Pots   Potting Soil   Seeds or Flowers

We would like the children to be able to hand the flowers out themselves. We can do this in two ways. Each child can take a flower pot home that you can then deliver to the senior center. Or, if you are available on _____ we can meet at the senior center at _____ A.M/P.M.

Please let us know what you prefer by this date: _____.

Thank You!

Military Cards & Care Packages

www.operationgratitude.com has information on sending cards and care packages. They have lists for donations you can print out. This organization is on the BBB list of accredited charities.

www.packagesfromhome.com is another BBB accredited charity where you can send packages and letters. They also have lists of what is needed and where to send packages on their website.

Attach the below flyer to the list of items you print out from whichever organization you choose to use.

Service Project

Dear Parents,

This month your preschoolers will be learning about serving others. They will be collecting items for military care packages. Please see the list of items we are looking for on the attached flyer.

Thank You for participating in this event!

Service Project

Dear Parents,

This month your preschoolers will be learning about serving others. They will be collecting items for military care packages. Please see the list of items we are looking for on the attached flyer.

Thank You for participating in this event!

Place this flyer in your church bulletin and place a printout from the organization you choose to use in the foyer where people can find it easily.

Service Project

This month our preschoolers will be learning about serving others. They will be collecting items for military care packages. Please see the list of items we are looking for in the foyer

Thank You for making this a successful event!

Service Project

This month our preschoolers will be learning about serving others. They will be collecting items for military care packages. Please see the list of items we are looking for in the foyer

Thank You for making this a successful event!

Service Project

This month our preschoolers will be learning about serving others. They will be collecting items for military care packages. Please see the list of items we are looking for in the foyer

Thank You for making this a successful event!

Operation Christmas Child

Many churches participate in this organization every year. If your church is one of them, have families bring donated items to the church and let the preschoolers pack the boxes.

If your church doesn't participate in this, but you would like your preschoolers to, visit http://www.samaritanspurse.org/what-we-do/operation-christmas-child to print out flyers, donation lists, where to send the shoe boxes or find drop off locations near you, and a lot of other great information.

Compassion International

Compassion International is another great organization to get involved with. If you have enough interest shown, you can have your class raise money through tithes and offerings to sponsor a child.

If this seems too overwhelming, you can also collect funds for the Unsponsored Children's Fund. This collects donations for all the children who haven't been sponsored yet so they also get the things they need. This option can be a once a year event instead of an every month event.

Visit Compassion.com for more information on sponsoring a child.

For more information about the Unsponsored Children's Fund visit: http://www.compassion.com/church-engagement/child-help.htm

There is also an option for raising money for clean water. You can find that here: http://www.compassion.com/church-engagement/water-aid.htm

Helping the Homeless

There are a lot of things you can do to help the homeless.

1. You can collect food for your local food bank.

2. Find out if your local shelters accept homeless kits and have the kids put together packets of toiletries.

3. Collect warm clothes to donate to the homeless.

4. Collect board games for the homeless shelters.

Other Service Project Ideas

1. Collect items for shelter animals.

2. Valentine's Cards for Senior Citizens.

3. Collect School Supplies for Kids in Need.

4. Collect old DVD's and games for a children's hospital.

5. Donate gently used stuffed animals to Police or Fire Departments for children in emergencies.

General parent flyer for service projects.

Service Project

Dear Parents,

This month your preschoolers will be learning about serving others. They will be collecting items for _____.

Thank You for participating in this event!

Service Project

Dear Parents,

This month your preschoolers will be learning about serving others. They will be collecting items for _____.

Thank You for participating in this event!

Service Project

Dear Parents,

This month your preschoolers will be learning about serving others. They will be collecting items for _____.

Thank You for participating in this event!

General service project flyer for bulletins.

Service Project

This month our preschoolers will be learning about serving others. They will be collecting items for _____. Please see the list of items we are looking for in the foyer.

Thank You for making this a successful event!

Service Project

This month our preschoolers will be learning about serving others. They will be collecting items for _____. Please see the list of items we are looking for in the foyer.

Thank You for making this a successful event!

Service Project

This month our preschoolers will be learning about serving others. They will be collecting items for _____. Please see the list of items we are looking for in the foyer.

Thank You for making this a successful event!

ACKNOWLEDGEMENTS

I would like to thank the preschooler teachers at New Creation Church who patiently stuck with me as I created and modified this curriculum as well as for the comments and feedback that made it that much better.

To my husband Craig, and my Mom, Sue; thank you for taking the time to read through this and double check everything for me!

To those in my writers group who took the time to read through parts of this book and give me feedback, Thank you!

For all the wonderfully creative people out there who inspired the crafts, games and activities found in this book, thank you for sharing your creativeness with the world.

Last, but never least, thank you God for creating a desire in me to serve the little ones and for dropping ideas for this book into my heart and making it a passion in me.